Contents

BEADED CHAINS & ROPES

Create Easy-to-Wear Jewelry Using Popular Stitches

Karin Van Voorhees

KALMBACH BOOKS

Kalmbach Books
21027 Crossroads Circle
Waukesha, Wisconsin 53186
www.JewelryandBeadingStore.com
© 2015 Kalmbach Publishing Co.

Published in 2015

19 18 17 16 15   1 2 3 4 5

Manufactured in China

ISBN: 978-1-62700-085-7

EISBN: 978-1-62700-086-4

Some material in this book has appeared previously in *Bead&Button* magazine. Bead&Button is registered as a trademark.

Editor: Karin Van Voorhees

Book Design: Elizabeth Weber

Technical Editor: Jane Danley Cruz

Illustrator: Kellie Jaeger

Photographers: James Forbes, William Zuback

Library of Congress Control Number: 2014950474

Introduction

Beaded ropes and chains—often cast in a supporting role for spectacular pendants, focals, or embellishment—have stepped forward to the limelight in this new compilation. Cast aside the utilitarian aspect of these jewelry mainstays, and focus instead on the many creative ways to stitch these lush lengths.

The 27 designs in this book explore a variety of stitches and stitch combinations that create luxurious rope-style jewelry, which is equally at home on the neck or wrist. The designs leave plenty of room for customization both in length and bead shapes, colors, and finishes. With eleven techniques and many variations—including herringbone, peyote, right-angle weave, spiral rope, St. Petersburg chain, bead crochet, and kumihimo—you'll have fun experimenting with familiar stitches or learning new ones as you create beautiful jewelry.

Each project is identified by stitch. All are explained in detail in the Basics section at the end of the book; take a moment before beginning a project to brush up on your basic skills, if needed.

Twenty contributing designers share projects in these pages in styles ranging from classic to contemporary and in difficulty from easy to advanced.

First published in this volume are new projects from Julia Gerlach, Jane Danley Cruz, Linda Gettings, Beth Stone, Anna Elizabeth Draeger, Isabella Lam, Carolyn Cave, Adele Rogers Recklies, and Rebecca Ann Combs. We asked these leading designers to create projects that used the newest bead shapes and finishes, as well as popular rope and chain stitching techniques.

We are fortunate to feature such interesting work. Please take the time to read about all the designers and their accomplishments on the contributors' page and to visit their respective websites to see more of their stunning work.

Projects

Bumps on a Rope

Add tiny "bumps" to a herringbone rope with 15º seed beads, and stitch accent pearl clusters for a classic necklace. Make this necklace with or without a favorite pendant.

designed by Julia Gerlach

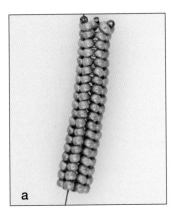

a

b

c

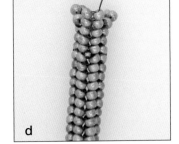

d

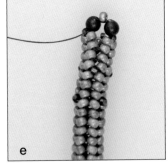

e

f

g

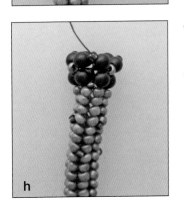

h

materials

both projects
- **2** bead caps
- clasp
- beading needles, #12
- beading thread

necklace with pendant
- electroformed glass and filigree pendant, Tammy Rae Wolter (www.tammyrae.com)
- 3mm crystal pearls
  18 cream
  72 bronze
- **12–14** 6mm crystal pearls (light bronze)
- 11º Seed beads
  5 g color A (metallic steel blue)
  1 g color B (purple)
- 1 g 15º seed beads (bronze)

necklace without pendant
- 3mm crystal pearls
  24 color D (cream)
  96 color C (petrol)
- 11º seed beads
  5 g color A (Caribbean mix)
  1 g color B (bronze)
- 1 g 15º seed beads (bronze)

Rope

1 On a comfortable length of thread and leaving an 8-in. (20cm) tail, make a ladder using six color A 11º seed beads. Form the ladder into a ring by sewing through the first and last beads.

2 Work in rounds of tubular herringbone stitch as follows:

Rounds 1–3: Work three rounds using As.

Round 4: Work a round using an A, a 15º seed bead, and an A for each stitch **(photo a)**.

Round 5: Work a round using As, skipping the 15ºs in the previous round. For each stitch, be sure to push the 15º in the previous round to the outside of the tube **(photo b)**.

Rounds 6–9: Work four rounds using As.

Round 10: Pick up two As, and sew down through the next A in the previous round. Pick up a 15º, and sew up through the next A **(photo c)**. Repeat these two stitches twice, and step up through the first A added in the round **(photo d)**.

Rounds 11–12: Work two rounds using As and skipping the 15ºs in round 10. As you stitch, make sure to push the 15ºs to the outer surface of the tube.

Rounds 13–48: Repeat rounds 4–12 four times.

Round 49: Repeat round 4.

3 Work a pearl cluster: Pick up a color C 3mm pearl, a color B 11º seed bead, and a C, and sew through the next 15º in the previous round **(photo e)**. Repeat this stitch twice to complete the round, and step up through the first C and B added in this round **(photo f)**.

4 Pick up a C, a 15º, and a C, and sew through the next B in the previous round **(photo g)**. Repeat this stitch twice to complete the round, and step up through the first C and 15º added in the round **(photo h)**.

5 Pick up two As, and sew through the 15º your thread exited at the start of this step and the following C, B, C, and 15º **(photo i)**. Repeat this stitch twice, and step up through the first A added in this round.

6 Sewing through the As added in the previous round, work a round of herringbone using As, being sure to snug up the beadwork to eliminate any gaps **(photo j)**. Sew down through the nearest column of As to exit a 15º added in the last round of pearls.

7 Pick up a 15º, a color D 3mm pearl, and a 15º, and sew through the opposite B **(photo k)**. Pick up a 15º, sew back through the D, pick up a 15º, and sew through the 15º your thread exited at the start of this step **(photo l)**. Sew through the beadwork to exit the next 15º in the round.

8 Repeat step 7 twice, and then sew through the nearest column of As to exit the end round.

9 Work two more rounds of herringbone with As.

10 Work as in rounds 10–12, and then work rounds 4–12 either once or twice, depending on how long you want the segments between the pearl clusters to be. End with round 4. In my necklace using seed beads, I did three repeats for a 1⅝-in. (4.1cm) segment. In my necklace using seed beads, I did two repeats for a 1-in. (2.5cm) segment.

11 Repeat steps 3–10 to create the desired number of clusters. If you plan to add a pendant, work about 1 in. (2.5cm) of plain herringbone without 15ºs where the pendant will hang. String the pendant onto the rope before making the pearl cluster that follows the center segment.

12 Work as in rounds 4–11 to create a mirror image of the starting end. Work one more round of herringbone using As, and then sew through the last round following a ladder stitch thread path.

Clasp

1 Pick up an end cap, one or more 6mm pearls if desired, seven 15ºs, and a clasp. Skip the last six 15ºs, and sew back through the first 15º picked up, the 6mm(s), and the end cap, and sew into the end of the rope, exiting several rows from the end of the rope.

2 Sew back through the beadwork, and retrace the thread path through the clasp connection a few times. End the thread.

3 Repeat steps 1 and 2 at the other end of the necklace.

ELEGANT ENDING Finish the stitched portion with end caps, and string a pearl extension.

Four Stitches;
One Stunning Rope

Tubes of regular and twisted herringbone and
brick stitch are an excellent base for square
stitched accents. Make an odd-count peyote bail
to support an art-glass bead.

designed by Michelle Bevington

NECKLACE A

NECKLACE B

materials

necklace A or B 16 in. (41cm)

- art-glass bead approx. 1½ in. (3.8cm) (Brendan Blake, etsy. com/shop/bbglassart)
- cylinder beads
  13 g color A
  6 g color B
  5 g color C
- 1 g 15º seed beads, color A
- 2 silver beads
- 2 silver spacers
- clasp
- 2 in. (5cm) 18- or 20-gauge wire
- 2½-in. (6.4cm) 22-gauge headpin
- Nymo D
- nylon cord (optional)
- beading needles, #12
- chainnose pliers
- roundnose pliers
- wire cutters

Base

On 3 yd. (2.7m) of thread, leave a 12-in. (30cm) tail, and pick up two color A cylinder beads. Make a bead ladder eight beads long. Join the beads into a ring, sewing through the first bead in the ladder and then back into the last bead.

Necklace A

1 Work in tubular herringbone stitch as follows:

Rounds 2–5: color B cylinder beads

Round 6: color A cylinder beads

Rounds 7–13: color C cylinder beads

Round 14: Bs

Round 15: As

Round 16: Bs

Rounds 17–23: Cs

Round 24: As

Rounds 25–29: Bs

Round 30: As.

When you complete the row, zigzag back through the beads to mimic a bead ladder **(photo a)**. This will become the first row of your brick stitch section.

Rounds 31–34: Work in brick stitch **(photo b)** using As.

Rows 35–39: Treating the last row of brick stitch as if it were the initial ladder, work five rounds of herringbone with Bs.

2 Repeat rounds 6–39 seven times. Repeat rounds 6–30.

3 Refer to "Ending the tubes" and "Pendant."

Necklace B

1 Work in tubular herringbone stitch as follows:

Rounds 2–31: color A cylinder beads

Rounds 32–48: color B cylinder beads

Rounds 49–68: As

Rounds 69–85: Bs

Rounds 86–120: As. This will be the center point of the necklace. Make the second half of the tube to mirror the first by working 34 rounds of As, 17 rounds of Bs, 20 rounds of As, 17 rounds of Bs, and 31 rounds of As. Zigzag through the last round to mimic the ladder base.

2 Refer to "Finishing," "Square stitch embellishment," and "Pendant."

Finishing

If your tube is too soft to support the bail, slide nylon cord through the center before finishing the ends.

1 With the thread exiting the ladder round, pick up an A and sew through the next A **(photo c)**. Repeat around, and step up through the first new A.

2 Work a round of tubular peyote stitch, picking up one A and sewing through the next A **(photo d)**. Continue to complete the round. Step up through the new A.

A ☐
B ■

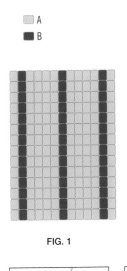 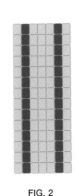

FIG. 1   FIG. 2

FIG. 3

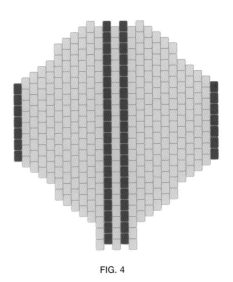

FIG. 4

  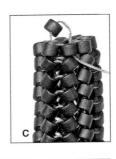  

a   b   c   d   e

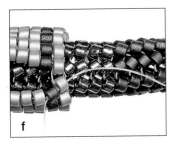 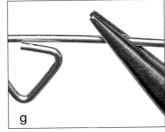  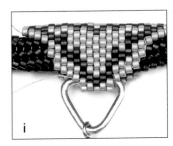

f   g   h   i

3 Work a second round of peyote with As. Work two rounds of peyote with 15º seed beads.

4 Retrace the last round to reinforce it, exiting a 15º. Pick up enough 15º to fit through the loop of one half of the clasp. Sew through the opposite 15º on the last round **(photo e)**. Reinforce the loop of 15º with a second thread pass.

5 Secure the thread with half-hitch knots, and trim.

6 Repeat steps 1–5 on the other end of the necklace.

Square Stitch Embellishment

1 On 2 yd. (1.8m) of thread, make a square stitch section that is 13 beads wide and 14 rows long **fig. 1**. Repeat to make four sections.

2 Wrap the section around the tubular herringbone sections, and stitch the two ends together with a square stitch thread path **(photo f)**. You may have to adjust the number of rows to accommodate the herringbone tube.

3 Secure the tails with half-hitch knots, and trim.

4 Refer to **fig. 2** to make two square stitch embellishments that are seven beads wide and 14 beads long. Attach them to ends of the tubes as in steps 2 and 3.

Pendant
Art-glass bead

1 On a headpin, string a silver bead, a spacer, the art-glass bead, a spacer, and a silver bead. Make a wrapped loop.

2 Using 18- or 20-gauge wire, make a triangle with rounded corners **(photo g)**. Trim any excess wire.

3 Slide the pendant on the triangle and close the triangle **(photo h)**.

Peyote Bail

1 Refer to **fig. 3 or 4** to stitch an odd-count peyote bail.

2 Wrap the bail around the center of the herringbone tube, place the pendant on one end of the bail, and stitch the last row to the first row **(photo i)**. Retrace the thread path several times for security.

3 Secure the tails with half-hitch knots, and trim.

Supple Ropes

A repeating pattern of bugle beads and cylinder beads worked in herringbone stitch creates interesting surface texture on a graceful rope. Enjoy the rope as a necklace or bracelet. Finish both with a peyote stitch toggle clasp.

designed by Jill Wiseman

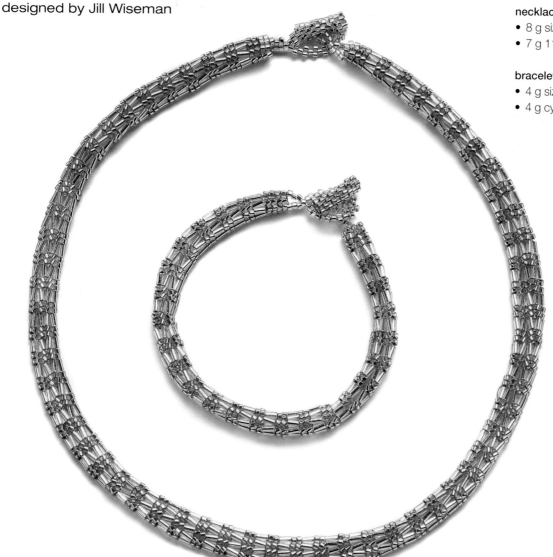

materials

both projects
- Fireline 6 lb. test
- beading needles, #10 or #12

necklace 16 in. (4 1cm)
- 8 g size 1 (3mm) bugle beads
- 7 g 11º cylinder beads

bracelet 7 in. (18cm)
- 4 g size 1 (3mm) bugle beads
- 4 g cylinder beads

Herringbone Rope

1 On 2 yd. (1.8m) of Fireline, pick up four cylinder beads. Go through again in the same direction, leaving a 6-in. (15cm) tail. Align the beads to start a ladder (**fig. 1, a–b**).

2 Continue the ladder with two cylinders per stitch until there is a total of eight stitches (**b–c**).

3 Connect the last stitch to the first to form a tube (**fig. 2, a–b**).

4 Work one round of herringbone: Pick up two cylinders, go down through the top cylinder in the adjacent stack, and come up through the next cylinder (**fig. 3, a–b**). Repeat around the tube.

5 To start the next round, step up by going through the top cylinder in the adjacent stack and the first cylinder in the first round (**fig. 4, a–b**). Continue in herringbone using cylinders (**b–c**), and step up as before.

6 Work the next round using bugle beads.

7 Continue stitching two rounds of herringbone using cylinders and one round using bugles until the tube is 1 in. (2.5cm) short of the desired length. End with three rounds of cylinders.

8 Pick up two cylinders, and go down through the top cylinder in the next stack (**fig. 5, a–b**). Go back through the top two cylinders in the previous stack (**b–c**), and continue through the top two in the next stack (**c–d**). This straightens the two sets of cylinders so they look like the ladder stitch row at the rope's start. Come up through the top cylinder in the next stack (**d–e**).

9 Pick up one cylinder, go back down through the top two cylinders in the previous stack, and come up through the top two in the next stack (**e–f**). Pick up one cylinder, go down through the top cylinder in the next stack, and come up through the top two cylinders in the previous stack. Go back down the top two cylinders in the next stack (**f–g**).

10 Repeat step 9 until you reach the start. Connect the last stitch to the first (**fig. 2, a–b**).

11 Secure the thread in the beadwork, and trim. Repeat with the tail at the starting end.

Clasp

1 On a comfortable length of Fireline, pick up a stop bead and leave a 6-in. tail. Pick up 10 cylinders, turn, and work back across the row in flat, even-count peyote stitch. Stitch a total of 10 rows.

2 Roll the peyote strip into a tube, and zip up the first and last rows (**photo a**).

3 Secure the thread, and trim. Remove the stop bead, and secure the other tail.

4 Start a new thread at one end of the rope, and exit any bead in the end row. Pick up six cylinders, go through two cylinders at the center of the peyote tube, and pick up two more cylinders. Go through the fourth cylinder of the first six, pick up three cylinders, and go through a bead on the rope's end row opposite the starting point (**photo b**).

5 Retrace the thread path twice, secure the thread, and trim.

6 For the loop, start a thread at the other end of the rope. Exit a bead in the end row that's in the same column of beads as the toggle connection. Pick up enough cylinders (about 27) to form a loop large enough to go over the toggle. Go through the fourth cylinder of the 27, pick up three cylinders, and go through a bead on the end row opposite the starting point (**photo c**).

7 Retrace the thread path three times. Work a row of peyote stitch around the loop (**photo d**). Secure the thread, and trim.

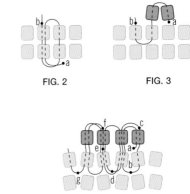

FIG. 1

FIG. 2

FIG. 3

FIG. 4

FIG. 5

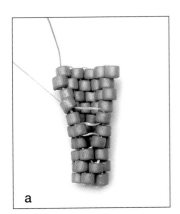

a

b

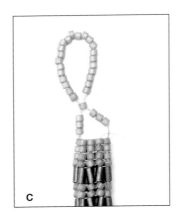

c

d

Twisted Lentils

Larger beads make a substantial rope that stitches up quickly. Using two sizes of beads and this unique stitching pattern emphasizes the "twist" in twisted tubular herringbone. Whether you choose the bracelet length or a longer necklace, you'll find this rope comfortable and easy to wear.

designed by Linda Gettings

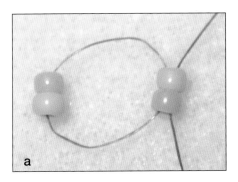

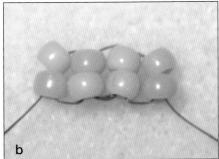

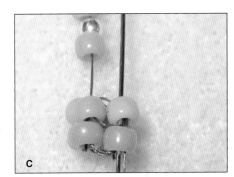

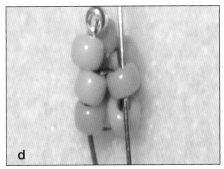

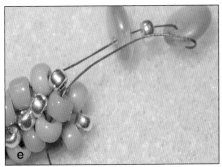

materials

all projects

- 8º (48 per in.) and 11º (28 per in.) seed beads in **2** colors (or 6ºs and 8ºs—see alternate)
- lentils (44 per in.)
- size 10 long tulip needle
- Fireline 8 lb. test
- clasp

1 On a comfortable length of thread, pick up four 8º seed beads to begin a ladder, leaving a 12-in. (30cm) tail.

2 Sew the first two beads again, and position the beads to form two two-bead columns **(photo a)**.

3 Working in ladder stitch, pick up two 8ºs, and sew through the previous stack and the new stack. Repeat this stitch once more **(photo b)**.

4 Sew up through the first stack to form a tube.

5 Pick up an 8º, an 11º and an 8º, and sew down through the adjacent stack of two 8º beads. **(photo c)**. Sew over and up through the top 8º only in the following stack **(photo d)**. The mantra is: pick up three beads (8º, 11º 8º), go down through two 8ºs and over and up through one 8º. Repeat for 6–8 in. (15–20cm) before switching to lentils. Do not sew through the 11º at any time.

Switching to Lentils

6 Exit an 8º and pick up a lentil, an 11º, and a lentil **(photo e)**. Work as in step 5, but with these **(photo f)** to create the twist.

Finishing

7 Repeat steps 1–5 to complete the neck-lace, but in the last two rounds eliminate the 11º. Sew through the final 8ºs to tighten the end of the tube before adding the closure.

ALTERNATE STYLE This bracelet uses 6ºs and 8ºs instead of 8ºs and 11ºs before switching to the lentil twist. Begin with 8ºs and 11ºs for 1 in. (25.5mm), then switch and stitch 3 in. (7.6cm) or more of the lentil twist. End the bracelet with 8ºs and 11ºs for 1 in. and add a clasp.

Floral Finery

Combine Russian leaves, petite petals, and twisted tubular herringbone rope with bud-like increases, fringe, and art beads to make one of two necklaces. Once you've mastered the techniques, there's no limit to the combinations.

designed by Mary Carroll

FIG. 1

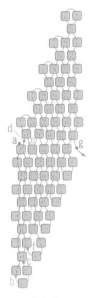

FIG. 2

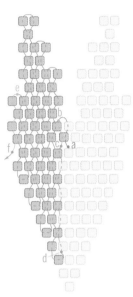

FIG. 3

materials

both projects
- beading thread, size D
- flexible beading wire, .014
- beading needles, #12
- crimping pliers
- wire cutters

pink lariat 38 in. (97cm)
- **10** 8mm round beads
- **3** 6mm round beads
- **21** 3mm bicone crystals
- 11º cylinder beads
  50 g color A
  8 g color B
- 8 g 15º or 11º seed beads
  (optional)
- 4 g 15º seed beads
- **4** crimp beads

green necklace 20 in. (51cm)
- **2** 5mm art-glass bead
- **4** 8mm round beads
- **4** 4mm round beads
- **9** 3mm round beads
- 30 g 11º cylinder beads
- 11º seed beads
- clasp
- **4** crimp beads

Pink Lariat
Inner Petals

1 Attach a stop bead to the center of 1 yd. (.9m) of thread, and pick up 22 color B 11º cylinder beads. Turn, and begin working in even count peyote stitch until you have a total of five rows.

2 Sew through the beadwork to exit the fourth B from the end of the last row **(fig. 1, a–b)**.

3 Work in peyote stitch, making a decrease turn at the end of each row for five rows: Stitch to the end of the row, exiting the last B **(b–c)**. Sew under the thread bridge between the B your thread exited and the adjacent B, and sew back through the B your thread exited and the last B added **(c–d)**. Repeat **(d–e)** four more times, ending with a three-bead row. End the thread.

4 Remove the stop bead from the tail, and exit the fourth up-bead from the end on the other side of the petal. Repeat step 3 to complete the petal.

5 Repeat steps 1–4 to make three more petals.

6 Use a ladder stitch thread path to join the two Bs at the narrow end of each petal so the petals form a circle **(photo a)**.

7 Repeat steps 1–6 twice.

Outer leaves

1 Attach a stop bead to the center of 1 yd. (.9m) of thread, and pick up 10 color A cylinder beads **(fig. 2, a–b)**.

2 Pick up two As to make the turn, and work across the row in peyote stitch using one A in each stitch **(c–d)**.

3 Make an increase at the end of the row by picking up three As. Snug them up to the beadwork, then skip the last two As, and sew back through the first A just picked up **(d–e)**. Stitch back across the row in peyote stitch, stopping one stitch short of the end of the row **(e–f)**.

4 Repeat steps 2 and 3 **(f–g)** four times.

5 Remove the stop bead. Pick up an A, and sew up through the outer A of the first increase **(fig. 3, a–b)**. Pick up an A, turn, and sew down through the first A picked up in this step **(b–c)**. Work across the row in peyote stitch, stopping one stitch short of the end of the row **(c–d)**.

6 Repeat steps 2 and 3 four times.

a

7 Sew through the beadwork to exit a top up-bead on the inside of the V. Work in ladder stitch to add a B and connect it to the corresponding up-bead on the other side of the V **(photo b)**. This will curve the leaf, giving it a cupped shape. Repeat to connect the other up-beads inside the V.

8 Repeat steps 1–7 to make a total of 12 outer leaves.

Rope

1 Cut a piece of beading wire 6 in. (15cm) longer than the desired finished length of your lariat. At one end, string a crimp bead, a 6mm round bead, and a cylinder bead. Go back through the 6mm and crimp bead, and crimp the crimp bead. String a set of inner petals so they cover the 6mm, and the long wire extends from the join at the top of the petals **(photo c)**.

NOTE: I graduated the colors in the ropes of my green necklace and used a second color for one of the outer leaves.

2 If desired, string 11º or 15º seed beads along the length of the wire, interspersing 6mm and 8mm round beads where you would like to add bulges to the rope. Otherwise, leave the wire bare, and slip the 6mms and 8mms into place before starting the decreases for the bulges. This rope has bulges three rows from the flower, four rows after the first bulge, and 2½ in. (6.4cm), 8¾ in. (22.2cm), 9¾ in. (24.8cm), and 24 in. (61cm) from the flower.

3 Using the ladder-stitched beads that join the inner petals as a base, work two rounds of tubular herringbone using As.

4 Work in twisted tubular herringbone to the point where you would like a bulge to begin. Work the first stitch of the next round, and pickup an A before sewing up through the top bead in the next column. Repeat around, and step up **(fig. 4, a–b)**.

5 Work two rounds of tubular herringbone, but pick up two As after each stitch **(b–c)**.

6 Work two rounds of tubular herringbone, picking up three As after each regular stitch **(c–d)**. If you are surrounding an 8mm bead, work one more round with three As after each regular stitch. If you are adding the 6mm or 8mm beads as you stitch, place the bead in the cup of the bulge now.

7 Work two rounds of tubular herringbone, but decrease by picking up two beads after each regular stitch.

8 Work a round of tubular herringbone with one cylinder after each regular stitch. Step up, and resume working in twisted tubular herringbone until you reach the point where you'll add the next bulge.

9 Work in twisted tubular herringbone using As until the rope is about 6 in. (15cm) short of the desired finished length, ending and adding thread as needed and stitching bulges as desired. Do not end the thread.

Split End

1 Repeat steps 1–8 of "Pink lariat: Rope" for each of the two remaining flowers, with these changes: Cut only a 7-in. (18cm) piece of beading wire for each flower. Stitch one rope to 2 in. (5cm) and the other to 3 in. (7.6cm), adding bulges as desired.

2 On one short rope, stitch two rounds of tubular herringbone, but do not add beads to one pair of stacks; stitch through the existing beads instead, leaving a notch in the end of the round. You should have three pairs of stacks in the end round. End the thread.

3 On the other short rope, stitch one round of tubular herringbone skipping a stack of beads, and two rounds skipping the same stack plus an adjacent stack. You should have two pairs of stacks in the end round.

4 Join the two ropes by stitching them together using a herringbone thread path: Position the two ropes so the notches are together, and stitch around both ropes using a herringbone thread path and skipping the short rows **(photo d)**.

5 Slide an 8mm bead over both wires, and stitch a bulge over it, as in steps 4–8 of "Rope."

6 Trim the wires as necessary so you can line up the end rounds of each rope. Stitch the ropes together using a herringbone thread path. End the threads.

Finishing

1 Attach a stop bead to a comfortable length of thread, leaving a 6-in. (15cm) tail, and sew through the cylinder bead inside one of the flowers. Pick up 1 in. (2.5cm) of 15º seed beads, a 3mm bicone crystal, and a 15º. Skip the last 15º and sew back through the 3mm, the 15º, and the cylinder. Repeat to add six more fringes, and end the working thread and tail. Repeat to add fringe to the other flowers.

2 Add a comfortable length of thread to the rope, exiting the beadwork where the rope meets the inner petals. Add one outer leaf at a time, sewing between the As on the leaf and the As on the rope in a herringbone thread path, until there are four leaves surrounding the rope. End the thread. Repeat to finish the remaining flowers.

Green Necklace

1 On a comfortable length of thread, leave a 6-in. (15cm) tail, and begin working in ladder stitch using 11º cylinder beads until your strip is eight beads long. Join the ends into a ring.

2 Work in twisted tubular herringbone stitch until the rope is 8½ in. (21.6cm) long, ending and adding thread as needed. End the tail, but do not end the working thread.

3 Cut a 15-in. (3 8cm) piece of beading wire, and string a crimp bead, a 4mm round bead, and half of the clasp. Go back through the 4mm and crimp bead, and crimp the crimp bead.

4 String a 4mm and an 8mm round bead on the wire, and then string the rope, ladder-end first.

5 Work the first half of an 8mm bulge as in steps 4–6 of "Pink lariat: Rope." String an 8mm on the wire, and work the second half of the bulge as in steps 7 and 8 of "Rope."

6 String a crimp bead, the art-glass bead, an 8mm, a 3mm round bead, and an 11º seed bead on the beading wire. Skip the 11º, and go back through the other beads, pulling them up to the beadwork. Crimp the crimp bead, and trim the tail.

7 Work in tubular herringbone until the crimp bead is covered and the beads meet the top of the art-glass bead. End the thread.

8 Work steps 1–7 of "Pink lariat: Outer leaves" to make four outer leaves.

9 To make the small leaves that decorate the herringbone rope, follow the instructions for "Pink lariat: Outer leaves," but pick up six cylinders in step 1 instead of 10.

10 Repeat steps 1–4 to begin the second half of the necklace.

11 To taper the end of the necklace, work a round of twisted tubular herringbone, but for one stitch, pick up a single cylinder instead of two cylinders. Work the next round,

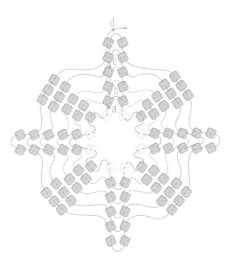

FIG. 4

and sew through the single cylinder instead of working the stitch. Work two rounds, skipping over the stitch with the single cylinder, and sewing into the next stitch.

12 Repeat step 11 to decrease the rope by another stitch. Continue working in two-stitch-per-round twisted tubular herringbone until the tail is long enough to wrap around the other rope several times.

13 String a crimp bead on the beading wire so it sits inside the rope, and go through a cylinder inside the rope. Go back through the crimp bead, taking care that the rope is loose enough to coil, and crimp it.

14 Work one more round of tubular herringbone, and sew through the beads in the last round to pull them tight together. End the thread.

15 Attach the outer leaves to the rope above the art-glass bead as in step 2 of "Pink lariat: Finishing."

16 Wind the tapered rope around the other rope above the art-glass bead, and use the tail to tack it in place. Use the tails from the small leaves to tack them to the ropes as desired. Sew 3mms to the top of the small leaves as desired. End all of the threads.

Two-Tone Helix

I don't have a favorite beading stitch, but right now, I'm crazy for herringbone. With that on the brain, I envisioned this twisting design and sketched it. This deceptively simple bracelet is now one of my favorites. Try mixing up different colors and sizes of beads. After all, that's where the fun is!

designed by Linda Gettings

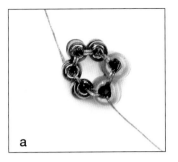
a

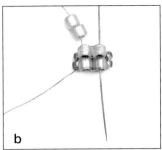
b

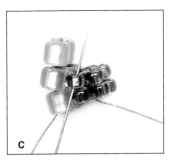
c

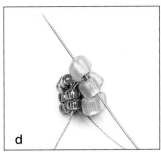
d

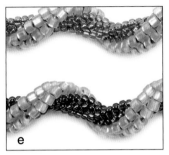
e

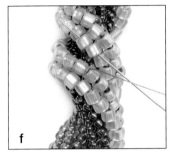
f

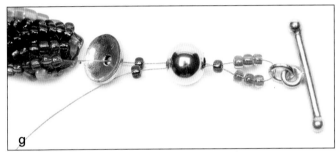
g

Instead of using 11º seed beads in two colors to get a two-tone interior twist (as in the black, gold, and blue bracelets), try using both sets of 11º's in a single color, as in the green and bronze version.

Single Twists

1 Thread a needle on a comfortable length of Fireline, leaving an 8-in. (20cm) tail. Stitch a ladder two beads tall and six beads wide, making the first two bead stacks using 8º seed beads, and the next four bead stacks using color A 11º's.

2 Join the ladder into a ring by sewing down through the first pair of beads and then back up through the last pair. Sew back through the first stack again to exit an 8º **(photo a)**.

3 To begin the first round of twisted herringbone, pick up two 8º's, and sew down into the two 8º's of the next stack of the base **(photo b)**. Sew up through the top A of the next stack **(photo c)**. Pick up two As, sew down into the two As

of the next base stack, and sew up through the top A of the next stack. Pick up two As and repeat once to complete the round, sewing up through the top two 8º's of the next stack to step up for the next round **(photo d)**.

4 Repeat step 3 to make a twisted herringbone rope that is approximately 7½ in. (19.1cm) long. Secure the tails with a few half-hitch knots between beads, and trim.

5 Repeat steps 1–4 to make another strand of the same length using 8º's and color B 11º's **(photo e)**.

Joining

1 Twist the two strands together, making sure that their ends line up.

2 Secure 1 yd. (.9m) of Fireline in one of the twists, and exit an end 8º. Sew through two or three 8º's, then cross over to the corresponding 8º on the other twist, and sew through two or three 8º's on that side. Continue

like this, sewing back and forth between the twists to connect them **(photo f)**. Secure the tails, and trim.

3 Repeat step 2 to connect the now aligned inside 11º's, sewing through three to five beads at a time on each side. Use chainnose pliers to maneuver the needle if needed. Secure the tails, and trim.

4 Secure 2 ft. (61cm) of Fireline in the beadwork, and exit one joined end. Pick up a bead cap, a B, a 6mm bead, a B, three As, half of a clasp, and three As. Sew through the B and the 6mm, and pick up a B **(photo g)**. Sew through the bead cap and into the beadwork. Pull tight, and retrace the thread path several times for support. To center the bead cap, sew into the beadwork at different points around the end of the twist. Secure the tails, and trim. Repeat on the opposite end with the other half of the clasp.

materials
bracelet 8 in. (20cm)
- **2** 6–8mm accent beads
- seed beads
  16 g 8º
  7 g 11º, in each of **2** colors: A, B
- **2** 10–12mm bead caps

clasp
- Fireline 6 lb. test
- beading needles, #12
- chainnose pliers (optional)

NOTE:
Tall, square-holed 8º's like those used here will create an angular look. If you prefer a more fluid helix, choose shorter, round-holed 8º's.

Linked Ladders

Make fast and easy bracelets with ladder stitch clusters.
Quick and satisfying, you'll want to own several.

designed by Julie Walker

materials

bracelet 7½ in. (19.1cm)
- 6 g 5º seed beads
- 2 g 11º seed beads
- clasp
- Fireline 6 lb. test
- beading needles, #12–#13

1 On a comfortable length of Fireline, pick up four 5º seed beads. Sew back through all four beads in the same direction, leaving a 12-in. (30cm) tail. Snug up the beads and adjust them so you have two pairs sitting side by side **(fig. 1, a–b)**.

2 Pick up two more 5ºs, sew through the previous pair, and sew back through the two beads just added **(b–c)**. Repeat to add a fourth pair **(c–d)**.

3 To join the four pairs of beads into a cluster, sew up through the first pair of beads, back down through the last pair, and back up through the first pair **(fig. 2)**.

4 Pick up 10 11º seed beads and four 5ºs. Sew back through the 5ºs again in the same direction.

5 Repeat steps 2 and 3 to make a second cluster. Sew back through an adjacent stack so your needle points toward the previous cluster **(photo a)**.

6 Line up the two clusters so the stacks are oriented the same way, and pick up 10 11ºs. Sew through the two 5ºs in the corresponding stack of the previous cluster **(photo b)**.

7 Sew through an adjacent stack of 5ºs, pick up 10 11ºs, and sew through the corresponding stack of 5ºs on the second cluster **(fig. 3, a–b)**.

8 Sew through the remaining 5ºs, pick up 10 11ºs, and sew through the corresponding 5ºs in the first cluster **(b–c)**.

9 Sew through an adjacent stack of 5ºs, the 11ºs, and the stack of 5ºs in the second cluster **(c–d)**.

10 Repeat steps 4–9 until your bracelet is approximately 1 in. (2.5cm) short of the desired length.

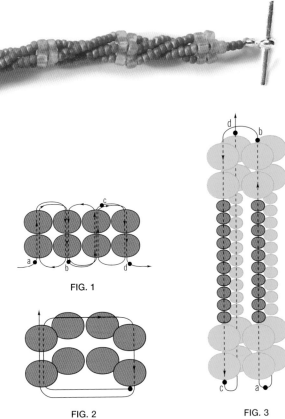

FIG. 1

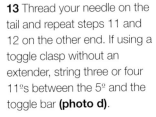

FIG. 2

FIG. 3

a

b

c

d

11 Pick up a 5º and a clasp half. Sew back through the 5º and sew into the 5º opposite where the thread is exiting **(photo c)**. Sew up an adjacent stack of 5ºs, and sew back through the end 5º and the clasp. Repeat the thread path several times to reinforce the connection.

12 Sew into the beadwork and make a half-hitch knot. Sew through a few beads, make another knot, sew through a few more beads, and trim.

13 Thread your needle on the tail and repeat steps 11 and 12 on the other end. If using a toggle clasp without an extender, string three or four 11ºs between the 5º and the toggle bar **(photo d)**.

Layered Ladders

Choose your style: Use pearls and gemstones to create the look of fine jewelry, as in the bejeweled bracelet at right; use drops and seed beads for a hint of sophistication, as in the center bracelet; or go for fresh casual with seed beads, as in the necklace to the left.

designed by Lisa Keith

FIG. 1

FIG. 2

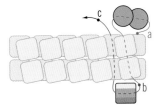

FIG. 3

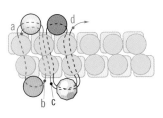

FIG. 4

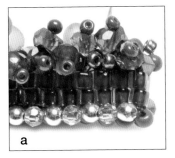

a

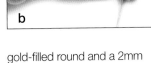

b

materials

all projects
- Fireline 4 lb. test
- beading needles, #12 or #13

bejeweled bracelet 8½ in. (21.6cm)
- **42–48** 3–4mm gemstone chips or faceted rondelles
- **42–48** 3–4mm top-drilled pearls or drop beads or keshi pearls
- **42–46** 2mm round gemstone beads
- **42–46** 2mm button pearls
- **63–69** 2mm round crystals
- **63–69** 2mm round gold-filled beads
- 1.5mm cube beads 5 g each of **2** colors: A, B
- 5 g 10º twisted hex-cut beads, color D
- 5 g 11º seed beads, color C
- 2 g 13º Charlottes
- clasp
- ½ in. (1.3cm) French (bullion) wire

curly necklace 16 in. (41cm)
- 5 g 11º cylinder beads, color A
- 5 g 11º seed beads, color B
- clasp
- ½ in. (1.3cm) French (bullion) wire

curly bracelet 7½ in. (19.1cm)
- 8 g 4mm fringe drop beads, color B
- 4 g 10º or 11º seed beads, color A
- 2 g 11º seed beads, color C
- 2 g 15º seed beads, color D
- clasp
- ½ in. (1.3cm) French (bullion) wire

Start with a double ladder base that twists as you stitch it, then decide how much you want to embellish your base—if at all.

Bejeweled Bracelet

Layer One: Twisted Double Ladder

1 On a comfortable length of Fireline, pick up four color A 1.5mm cube beads, and sew through all four beads again to form two stacks of two beads, leaving a 6-in. (15cm) tail.

2 Pick up two As, and sew down through the previous pair of As and up through the prior pair of As **(fig. 1)**.

3 Pick up two color B 1.5mm cube beads, and zigzag through the last two pairs of As **(fig. 2)**.

4 Repeat steps 2 and 3 until the band is the desired length, ending and adding thread as needed. You'll see the twist form after a few inches.

Layer two: Side Embellishments

Layer two follows the thread path between the ladders, and adds beads to hide the thread.

1 Exiting an A, pick up two color C 11º seed beads, and sew through the next pair of Bs **(fig. 3, a–b)**.

2 Pick up a color D 10º hex-cut bead, and sew through the next pair of As **(b–c)**.

3 Repeat steps 1 and 2 along the length of the bracelet.

Layer Three: Edge Embellishments

Layer three adds embellishment to each corner of the square.

1 Exiting an end C, pick up a 2mm pearl, and sew through the next pair of Cs **(fig. 4, a–b)**. Pick up a 2mm gold-filled bead, and sew through the pair of Cs your thread exited at the start of this step, the pearl, and the next pair of Cs **(b–c)**. Following a right-angle weave thread path, repeat along the band's length, alternating a pearl and a 2mm gemstone on one edge and a

gold-filled round and a 2mm crystal on the other **(c–d)**.

2 Sew through the beadwork to exit the end D on the other side. Pick up a 3–4mm pearl or drop bead, and sew through the next D **(fig. 5, a–b)**. Pick up a 3–4mm gemstone chip or rondelle and a 13º Charlotte, sew back through the gemstone, and sew through the previous D, the pearl, and the following D **(b–c)**. Following a right-angle weave thread path, continue to add a pearl or drop bead in each stitch along one edge and a gemstone and a Charlotte in each stitch along the other edge **(c–d)**.

3 Still working on the D surface, continue following a right-angle weave thread path through the Ds, but pick up two 13º Charlottes for each stitch on the edge with the gemstones **(photo a)**, and a C, a Charlotte, and a C for each stitch on the edge with the pearls or drops **(photo b)**. Position the new beads under the beads in the previous layer. This helps the gemstone and a pearl or drop embellishments stand up. Complete both edges.

4 Exiting the end hex-cut on the edge with the pearls or drops, sew through the pearl or drop toward the middle of the bracelet. Pick up a 2mm gold-filled bead or crystal, and sew through the next pearl or drop **(photo c)**. Repeat along the edge, inserting a 2mm gold-filled bead or crystal between each pair of pearls or drops.

Clasp

Exiting an end pair of As, pick up ¼ in. (6mm) of French wire and one half of the clasp, and sew through the end pair of As **(photo d)**. Retrace the thread path, and end the thread. Repeat at the other end of the bracelet with the tail.

Curly Necklace

1 Substitute 11º cylinder beads for the As and 11º seed beads for the Bs to make layer one of "Bejeweled bracelet."

2 Add a clasp as in "Bejeweled bracelet."

Curly Bracelet

1 Substitute 10º seed beads for the As and 4mm drops for the Bs to make layer one of "Bejeweled bracelet."

2 Work as in "Bejeweled bracelet: Layer two," using one color C 11º seed bead instead of two and three color D 15º seed beads instead of a 10º hex-cut.

3 Add a clasp as in "Bejeweled bracelet."

c

d

NOTE: For the modified ladder base, using the same size beads produces a blocky, gradual twist. The shape of the beads affects the twist too. Beads that fit together more tightly, like cylinders and cubes, form a somewhat angular twist. Pairing beads of different sizes creates a loopy spiral. To achieve this look, use the smaller beads as the As and the larger beads as the Bs. The thread shows in layer one, so if you are not adding embellishment, the thread color should be a design consideration.

Elegant Option The materials set the tone with this design. Pearls, crystals, and opulent seed bead finishes make a stunning statement.

It's a Wrap

I like to call right-angle weave (RAW)
"Really Awesome Weave!" Why?
Because this single-row version lends
itself to an infinite number of variations
with just a change of the beads or the
order of the beads used. Double-drilled
pearls add a wonderful accent, and the
peyote-stitched clasp is the
perfect seamless finish for this necklace
or multi-wrap bracelet.

designed by Beth Stone

materials

wrap bracelet or necklace, p. 29
- 6º seed beads, turquoise
- 8º seed beads, matte gold
- double-drilled pearls (Substitute any two-hole bead)

wrap bracelet or necklace, p. 30
- 11º seed beads
- 8º seed beads
- 6º seed beads
- CzechMates
- long drops
- 8º triangles
- Rullas
- lentil beads
- hand stitched button clasp

wrap bracelet or necklace, p. 31
- 11º seed beads
- 8º seed beads
- 6º triangles
- 8º triangles
- 11º triangles
- twin beads
- 3.4 mm drop beads
- 1.5 mm cube beads

Any beads can be used in any combination. The fun isn't in copying this bead for bead, but in trying new and interesting combinations!

These instructions are for right-angle weave. After you master the stitch, play with your beads to create your own version of my wrap bracelet or necklace. An easy way to think about the structure of right-angle weave is to think about the design of a room with each side representing either a floor, ceiling, or one of two walls. If you look at the diagram in step 2, bead #1 is the "ceiling," beads #2 and #4 are the "walls," and bead #3 is the "floor." For this project, you will be creating a string of "rooms," with each room alternating clockwise and counterclockwise. This concept will become clear as we work through these instructions.

1 On a comfortable length of thread, pick up a color A 11º seed bead, a color B 11º seed bead, a color C 11º seed bead, and a color D 11º seed bead **(fig. 1)**, and sew through the A again to form a ring, leaving a 6-in (15cm) tail.

2 Create a circle by passing your needle back through the first bead (#1) in the same direction it was originally strung **(fig. 2)**. The working thread and the tail thread will be coming out of the same bead, in opposite directions.

3 To begin the construction of each "room," your thread must exit a "wall" bead. Pass your needle through bead #2 red **(fig. 3)**.

4 Pick up three beads: #5 purple, #6 green, and #7 yellow. Pass your needle through bead #2 red, which becomes the common "wall" bead between the two "rooms" **(fig. 4)**.

5 Pass your needle through bead #5 purple (the floor) and bead #6 green (a wall bead) to position your thread to build the next room **(fig. 5)**.

6 Notice that the first "room" was created in a clockwise direction and the second "room" was created in a counterclockwise direction. This third "room" will again be created in a clockwise direction. Pick up beads #8 dark blue, #9 pink, and #10 red. Pass your needle through bead #6, which is the wall bead between the second room and the third room **(fig. 6)**.

7 Pass your needle through bead #8 dark blue (ceiling) and bead #9 pink (wall) to position your thread to build the next room **(fig. 7)**.

Mix it up! Once you master the basic RAW stitch, you can begin changing bead shape, size, and/or color. You can also begin using two or more beads for the floor and ceiling beads. Experiment, play and have fun creating your own work of art!

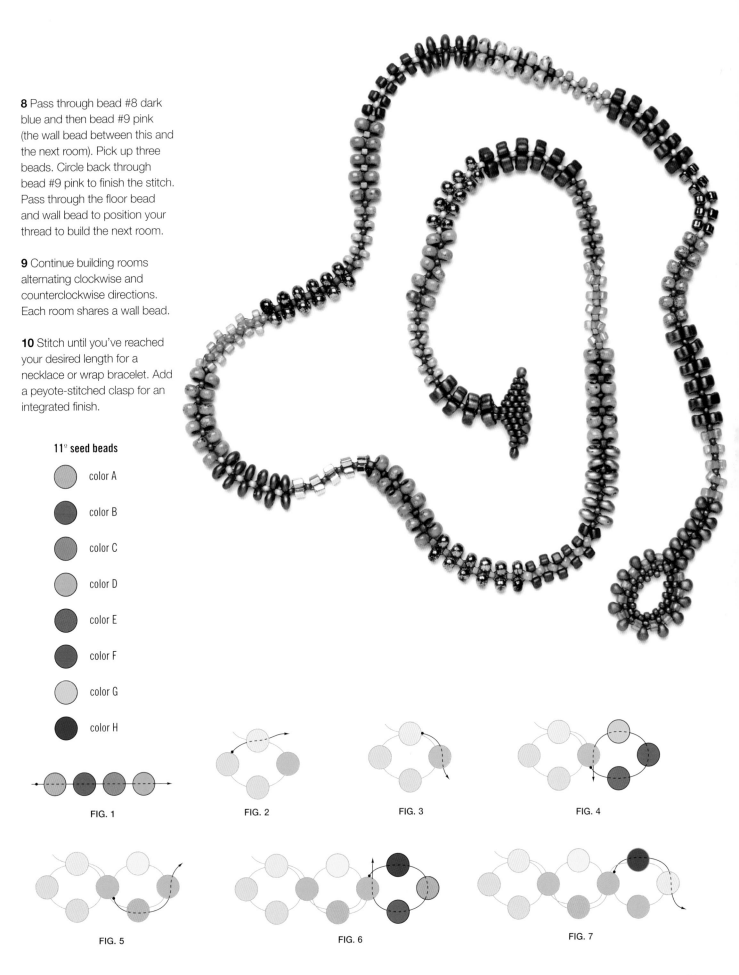

8 Pass through bead #8 dark blue and then bead #9 pink (the wall bead between this and the next room). Pick up three beads. Circle back through bead #9 pink to finish the stitch. Pass through the floor bead and wall bead to position your thread to build the next room.

9 Continue building rooms alternating clockwise and counterclockwise directions. Each room shares a wall bead.

10 Stitch until you've reached your desired length for a necklace or wrap bracelet. Add a peyote-stitched clasp for an integrated finish.

11° seed beads

color A

color B

color C

color D

color E

color F

color G

color H

FIG. 1

FIG. 2

FIG. 3

FIG. 4

FIG. 5

FIG. 6

FIG. 7

Power Trio

Embellish a
supple spine
of cubic
right-angle
weave with
sparkling
seed beads.
Stitch several
of these fun
bracelets to
wear together!

designed by
Isabella Lam

materials

pink bracelet 8 in. (20cm)
- 7–8 g 8º seed beads (Toho 2107, milky electric pink)
- 2–3 g 11º cylinder beads (Miyuki DBC0310, matte black)
- 2–3 g 15º seed beads (Toho 711, nickel-plated silver)
- **2** 10x11mm end caps (silver)
- clasp
- Fireline 6 lb. test
- beading needles, #11

blue bracelet colors:
- 8º seed beads (Toho 511F, metallic frosted Mediterranean blue)
- 11º cylinder beads (Miyuki DB0218, medium blue opaque luster)
- 15º seed beads (Toho 711, nickel-plated silver)

gold bracelet colors:
- 8º seed beads (Miyuki 551, gilt-lined opal)
- 11º cylinder beads (Miyuki DB002 7, metallic dark green iris cut)
- 15º seed beads (Miyuki 1421, dyed silver-lined golden olive)

purple bracelet colors:
- 8º seed beads (Toho 928, color-lined purple/rosaline AB)
- 11º cylinder beads (Miyuki DB0027, metallic dark green iris cut)
- 15º seed beads (Miyuki 551, gilt-lined opal)

pearl bracelet colors:
- 8º seed beads (Toho 592, antique ivory pearl Ceylon)
- 11º cylinder beads (Miyuki DB0042, silver-lined gold)
- 15º seed beads (Miyuki 313, cranberry gold luster)

Rope

1 On a comfortable length of Fireline, work a strip of three right-angle weave stitches using 8º seed beads and leaving a 6-in. (15cm) tail. Join the first and last stitches to form a ring: Exit an end 8º in the last stitch. Pick up an 8º, sew through the end 8º in the first stitch **(fig. 1, a–b)**, pick up an 8º, and sew through the end 8º in the last stitch **(b–c)**. Sew through the four 8ºs on the top and bottom of the cube.

2 Continue working in cubic right-angle weave, working off of the four top 8ºs in the previous cube: Exit a top 8º, pick up three 8ºs, and sew through the top 8º your thread just exited and the first 8º just picked up. For the next stitch, pick up two 8ºs, sew through the next top 8º, the side 8º in the previous stitch, and the two 8ºs just picked up.

For the third stitch, sew through the next top 8º, and pick up two 8ºs. Sew through the side 8º in the previous stitch, the third top 8º, and the first 8º just picked up. For the fourth stitch, pick up an 8º, and sew through the side 8º in the first stitch, the fourth top 8º, the side 8º in the previous stitch, and the 8º just picked up. To complete the cube, sew through the four new top 8ºs.

3 Repeat step 2 for the desired length, ending and adding thread as necessary. End the working thread and tail.

Embellishment

1 Add 2 yd. (1.8m) of Fireline to one end of the rope, exiting an end 8º. Pick up an 11º cylinder bead, and sew through the next end 8º in the same round

of the rope. Repeat this stitch three more times, and step up through the first cylinder picked up in this step **(fig. 2)**.

2 Pick up four 15º seed beads, a cylinder, and four 15º. Skip the next cylinder added in the previous round, and sew through the following cylinder **(fig. 3, a–b)**. Repeat this stitch, and step up through the first four 15º and cylinder picked up at the start of this step **(b–c)**.

3 Sew through the adjacent 8º in the next round of the rope that is parallel to the hole in the cylinder your thread is exiting **(c–d)**. Pick up a cylinder, and sew through the next 8º in the same round **(d–e)**, the center cylinder in the next stitch of the previous step **(e–f)**, and the next 8º in the same round of the rope **(f–g)**. Pick up a cylinder, and sew through the next 8º in the same round of the rope, the center cylinder added in the next stitch of the previous step, the following 8º in the same round of the rope, and the first cylinder picked up in this step **(g–h)**. This will ensure that the embellishment stitches line up.

4 Repeat steps 2 and 3 for the length of the rope, and end the thread.

Clasp

1 Add 12 in. (30cm) of thread to one end of the rope, and pick up an end cap, an 8º, three 15ºs, half of the clasp, and three 15ºs. Sew back through the 8º and the end cap, and continue into the rope. Retrace the thread path several times to secure, and end the thread.

2 Repeat step 1 on the other end of the rope.

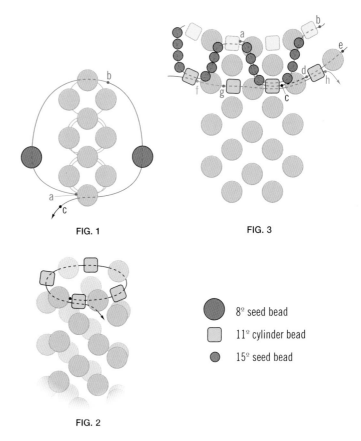

FIG. 1

FIG. 3

FIG. 2

○ 8º seed bead

▫ 11º cylinder bead

● 15º seed bead

Sparkle For a touch of glam, substitute 2mm round crystals for the cylinder beads.

Playful Pathways

Elevate your right-angle weave skills using two needles and a few of the fun new bead shapes now available, including O beads and two-holed beads. This intriguing pattern is surprisingly easy but never boring.

designed by Anna Elizabeth Draeger

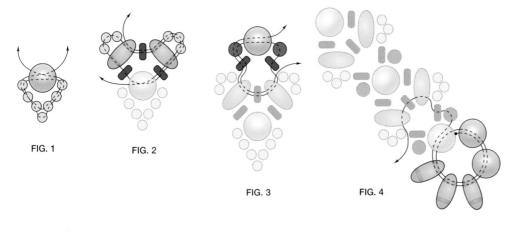

FIG. 1

FIG. 2

FIG. 3

FIG. 4

materials

Bracelet 7 in. (18cm)

- **20** 3mm Swarovski pearls or crystals
- **100** O beads
- **36** SuperDuo beads or two-hole lentils
- 4–5 grams 11º seed beads
- 4 grams 15º seed beads

Clasp

- **2** 6mm jump rings
- Fireline 6–8 lb. or other beading thread
- beading needles, #12

Bracelet

1 Thread a needle on each end of a 2-yd. (1.8m) length of thread. With one needle, pick up a 3mm pearl and seven 15º seed beads. Center the beads, and cross the other needle through the 3mm. Retrace the thread path with one needle to reinforce. Make sure both threads exit opposite sides of the 3mm **(fig. 1)**.

2 With one needle, pick up an O bead, a two-hole lentil or SuperDuo, and three 15ºs. Slide the beads down to the pearl. Sew through the open hole of the two-hole bead. Pick up an O bead, a two-hole bead, and three 15ºs. Snug up the beads, and sew through the open hole of the new two-hole bead. Pick up an O bead and

sew through the 3mm pearl again.

3 With the other needle, sew through the nearest O bead, two-hole bead, the following three 15ºs, the other hole of the two-hole bead, the next O bead, and corresponding hole of the following two-hole bead **(fig. 2)**. Repeat with the other thread.

4 With one needle, pick up an O bead, an 11º seed bead, a 3mm, an 11º, and an O bead. Sew back through the corresponding hole of the opposite two-hole bead, the next O bead, and the corresponding hole of the next two-hole bead **(fig. 3)**. With the other needle, sew through the beads to exit the new 3mm.

The thread should be exiting the 3mm on each side.

5 Repeat steps 2 and 3 until you reach the desired length, ending after completing step 3. With one needle, pick up three 15ºs. With the other needle, pick up four 15ºs. Cross the first needle through the fourth 15º just picked up with the other needle. Retrace the thread paths and end the tails.

Clasp

1 Open a 6mm jump ring, attach one half of the clasp and the seed bead loop at one end of the bracelet. Close the jump ring. Repeat on the other end.

Necklace

1 Work steps 1–4 of bracelet. Repeat steps 2 and 3, alternating two-hole lentil beads with SuperDuo beads in step 2 until you reach the desired center, ending after completing step 3.

2 Exit a 3mm and use either needle to pick up: two 3mms, SuperDuo, two-hole lentil, SuperDuo. Sew through the 3mm your thread first exited **(fig. 4)**. Retrace the ring several times, and end the threads.

3 For the second half, work as in step 1, but in the last repeat of step 3, sew through the existing 3mm (the second 3mm picked up in step 2) instead of picking up a new one. Retrace the thread path of the last unit, and end the threads.

Sweet detail The necklace features a delicate design in the center that casts the SuperDuos in a slightly different role.

Double the Fun

This rope is sure to become your go-to necklace when you want to display a pendant or other focal. Thin and supple, it is easy to stitch up and string through large bails. In addition, the double box technique adds texture, and the use of two-hole beads creates interest and substance so this rope is perfectly capable of standing on its own.

designed by Jane Danley Cruz

Rope

These instructions are for the necklace pictured at the bottom of this page. The necklace on p. 36 uses bicone crystals and half-Tilas.

First Layer

1 Thread a needle on each end of 3 yds. (2.7m) of Fireline, and center seven 11º seed beads on the thread. With each needle, pick up one hole of a Rulla bead.

2 With each needle, pick up four 11ºs. With one needle, pick up a 6º seed bead, and cross the other needle through it. **(fig. 1, a–b and aa–bb)**. With each needle, pick up four 11ºs and a Rulla **(b–c and bb–cc)**. This completes the first box in the chain.

3 For subsequent stitches: With each needle, pick up four 11ºs. With one needle, pick up a 6º, and cross the other needle through it. With each needle, pick up four 11ºs and a Rulla. Repeat this step for the length of the rope.

4 Once you're reached the desired length, with one needle, pick up seven 11ºs, and sew through the other hole of the last Rulla. With the remaining needle, sew through the seven 11ºs picked up with the other needle and the other hole of the last Rulla. Both needles will be pointing toward the starting end of the rope.

Second Layer

1 With each needle, pick up four 11ºs, sew through the 6º added in the "First layer," pick up four 11ºs, and sew through the corresponding hole of the next Rulla.

2 Work as in step 1 for the length of the rope to create a double layer of 11ºs.

3 Retrace the thread path through the seven-bead loop at the starting end of the rope, and end the threads.

Clasp

Open a jump ring, and attach a seven-bead loop at one end of the rope and half of the clasp. Close the jump ring. Repeat on the other end.

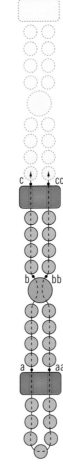

FIG. 1

materials

Necklace 24-in. (61cm)
- **34** Rulla beads
- **33** 6º seed beads
- 8–10 g 11º seed beads
- **2** 6mm jump rings
- toggle clasp
- Fireline 6 lb. test
- beading needles, # 10 or #11

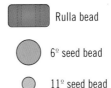

Rulla bead

6º seed bead

11º seed bead

Experiment! You have many options with this design. Substitute 6mm crystals for the 6º seed beads. Substitute SuperDuos, Twin beads, two-hole lentils, two-hole brick beads, or half-Tilas for the Rulla beads. If an organic look is more your style, choose beads with Picasso finishes.

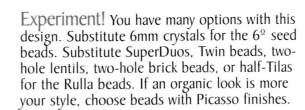

Twisted Sisters Spiral

Like climbing rungs on a ladder, stitch this supple serpentine rope step by step. It's fun and flexible, and you'll be surprised how quickly you progress.

designed by Isabella Lam

a

b

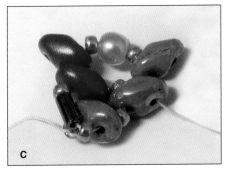

c

d

e

materials

Necklace 18 in. (46cm)

- **100** 3mm pearls
- **100** 2.5x5mm SuperDuo beads, color A
- **100** 2.5x5mm SuperDuo beads, color B
- 5 g 3mm bugle beads
- 5 g 15º seed beads
- **2** cones
- **2** split rings or jump rings
- Hook, toggle, or magnetic clasp
- Fireline 6 lb. or similar
- beading needles, #11

Let color be your guide Contrasting colors make a festive rope, while a monochromatic scheme is more subdued. You'll want to make a variety of these ropes in different lengths.

1 On a comfortable length of thread, string a stop bead leaving a 6-in. (15cm) tail. Sew through the stop bead twice to anchor.

2 Pick up a color A SuperDuo, a 15º seed bead, a color B Super-Duo, a 15º, an A, and a 15º, and sew through the open hole of the first A added **(photo a)**.

3 Pick up a 15º, a 3mm bugle, a 15º, and sew diagonally through the open hole of the B added in the previous step **(photo b)**.

4 Pick up a B, a 15º, a 3mm pearl, a 15º, and an A, and sew through the open hole of the nearest A **(photo c)**.

5 Repeat steps 2 and 3 **(photo d)** until you reach the desired length. End the threads **(photo e)** and add the cones and clasp.

New Spin on Spiral

I developed a variation on the traditional
approach to adding bead loops to embellish an
existing base. Instead of working a single row of
loops—as in spiral rope—I make a second pass
to hold the first round of loops in place. The result
is a thick, rich-looking rope with great body.

designed by Anna Elizabeth Draeger

materials

bracelet 8 in. (20cm)

- **58** 4mm Swarovski bicone crystals
- **57** seed pearls
- Seed beads
  10g 15º
  10g 11º
  5g 6º
- ⅞-in. (2.2cm) flower or button for clasp
- flexible beading wire, .014
- **2** crimp beads
- Silamide or Fireline, 6 lb. test
- beading needles, #13
- crimping pliers
- wire cutters

a

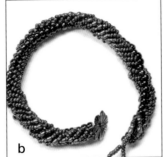

b

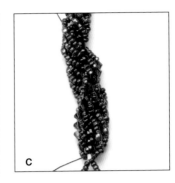

c

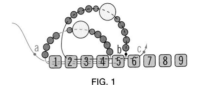

FIG. 1

FIG. 2

Base

1 String a crimp bead, an 11º seed bead, the flower or button clasp, and an 11º to 1½ in. (3.8cm) from the end of a 12-in. (31cm) piece of beading wire. Go back through the flower, the 11º, and the crimp bead. Crimp the crimp bead. Trim the tail.

2 String enough 6º seed beads to fit around your wrist.

3 String a crimp bead and enough 11ºs to encircle the widest part of the flower. Go back through the crimp bead and crimp it, leaving ⅛ in. (3mm) of space between the 6º and the crimp **(photo a)**.

Pearl Loops

1 Start a 3-yd. (2.7m) length of thread through the first four 6ºs on either end, leaving a 6-in. (15cm) tail.

2 Pick up four 11ºs, a 15º seed bead, a pearl, a 15º, and four 11ºs. Sew through beads one through five on the base **(fig. 1, a–b)** to complete the first loop and position the needle for the next loop. Push the first loop to one side.

3 Pick up four 11ºs, a 15º, a pearl, a 15º, and four 11ºs. Sew through beads two through six on the base **(b–c)**. Push this loop on top of the previous loop. Make sure the loops stack on top of each other and don't flop back and forth.

4 Repeat step 2, moving up one bead along the base for each loop added, until you exit the last 6º. The spiral doesn't take shape until the crystal loops are added **(photo b)**.

5 Secure the thread by sewing back through the last few loops added and tying half-hitch knots between a few of the beads. Repeat on the other end and trim the tails.

Crystal Loops

1 Start a new 3-yd. thread. Sew through the first three 6ºs on the same end you started the pearl loops. Leave a 6-in. (15cm) tail.

2 Pick up two 11ºs, a 15º, a crystal, a 15º, and two 11ºs. Sew back through base beads one through four **(fig. 2, a–b)**. to complete the first loop and position the needle for the next

loop. Push the crystal loop to the same side as the pearl loops.

3 Pick up two 11ºs, a 15º, a crystal, a 15º, and two 11ºs. Sew through base beads 2–6 **(b–c)**. Push this loop on top of the previous crystal loop **(photo c)**.

4 Repeat step 2 until you exit the last 6º. Work in the same direction as the pearl loops, pushing all the loops to one side.

5 Secure the tails with half-hitch knots and trim.

Pathway
Follow the path defined by the pearl loops to avoid splitting the loops down the middle.

Out for a Spin

While you're most likely to see lentil beads at
the end of a dangle, they really stand up and
get noticed in this project. Add them to a simple
spiral rope for a lavish, jewel-toned necklace.

designed by Carol Perrenoud

Rope

1 Using a comfortable length of Fireline, pick up four color A 11º seed beads, one color B 11º seed bead, one color A lentil, and one B 11º. Leaving a 10-in. (25cm) tail, tie a surgeon's knot as shown in **fig. 1, point a**. Go back through the four A 11ºs **(a–b)**.

2 Pick up an A 11º, a B 11º, a color B lentil, and a B 11º **(fig. 2, a–b)**. Go through the top three A 11ºs and the new A 11º just added **(b–c)**. Move the new lentil group over to the left so it's next to the first.

3 Repeat step 2, rotating your lentil colors, until your necklace is the desired length. My necklace is 30 in. (76cm).

Finish the ends

1 To make the loop closure, pick up 21 A 11ºs.

2 Go back through several As in the rope **(fig. 3, a–b)**. Secure the Fireline, and trim the tail.

3 On the other end of the necklace, thread a needle on the tail.

4 To make the flower, pick up three A 11ºs, a B 11º, an A lentil, and a B 11º **(fig. 4, a–b)**.

5 Go through the last A 11º in the core and the three new A 11ºs **(b–c)**.

6 Pick up a B 11º, a B lentil, and a B 11º **(fig. 5, a–b)**. Go back through the top three A 11ºs **(b–c)**.

7 Stitch three more lentil groups (rotating colors), always going through the top three A 11ºs. By going through the same As, the lentils will fan out into flower petals. The top of the flower is shown in **fig. 6**.

8 Go back down the core, and reinforce the connection by going through several petals and at least the first five core beads. Secure the Fireline and trim the tail.

materials

necklace 30 in. (76cm)

- **125** each of 6mm lentil beads: olive green, color A; purple, color B; amber, color C; cranberry, color D
- 30 g each of 11º seed beads: olive green, color A; purple, color B
- Fireline 6 lb. test
- beading needles, #12

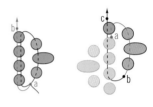
FIG. 1   FIG. 2

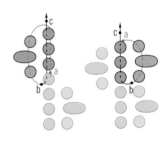
FIG. 3

FIG. 4   FIG. 5

FIG. 6

GO TO GREAT LENGTHS Wear your necklace at different lengths by making an easy extension. Make a spiral rope the desired length by following steps 1–3, but substitute color B 11ºs for the lentil beads. By finishing with a loop on one end and a flower on the other, you can connect the extension to the larger rope as shown in the photo, or wear it as a bracelet or anklet.

Grapevine Rope

This elegant, open-weave rope is one fashion accessory you're sure to love. Using the ever-popular two-hole beads (SuperDuos or twins) and seed beads, stitch this fabulous rope to wear alone or to display your favorite pendant.

designed by Carolyn Cave

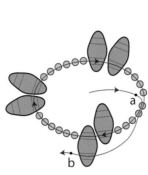

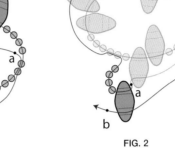

FIG. 1

FIG. 2

Super Duo bead

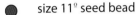
size 11º seed bead

15º seed bead

materials
- 32 g twin beads, opaque purple iris
- 11 g 15º seed beads, gold luster violet
- 1 g 11º seed beads, amethyst galvanized metallic (or any other purple shade)
- 5 5 x3 5mm leaf and twig toggle clasp, or other decorative clasp (Bead World, Edmonton)
- 2 10x5mm bead caps, silver
- 2 5mm jump rings, 18 gauge, silver
- 60cm (24 in.) 4mm rubber tubing
- Fireline, 10 lb. test, smoke
- beading needles, #12
- sharp scissors
- two pairs of pliers
- measuring tape

1 Add a stop bead on a comfortable length of thread, leaving a 12-in. (30cm) tail.

2 Pick up five 15ºs seed beads, two twin beads, six 15ºs, two twins, six 15ºs, two twins, and four 15ºs, and sew through the first two 15ºs again to form a ring. Continue through the open hole of the second twin just picked up **(fig. 1, a-b)**.

3 Pick up a twin and four 15ºs, skip the next 15º in the round below, and sew through the second and third 15º. Skip the next three 15ºs and sew through the open hole of the following twin. Repeat this stitch

once. Pick up a twin and four 15ºs, skip the 15º in the previous round, and sew through the second and third 15ºs and the open hole of the first twin added in this round **(fig. 2, a-b)**. The beads in the first round will begin to bunch together. The twin added in each stitch will swing around and make a "stair" with the one below it **(photo a)**.

4 Insert one end of the rubber tubing into the center of the ring. Pick up a twin and four 15ºs, skip the next 15º in the round below, and sew through the second and third 15ºs, and the open hole of the next twin in

the previous round **(photo b)**. Work around the rubber tubing, pushing the beads along.

Repeat step 4 until you have 181 rounds, or for the desired length. Add thread as needed. Trim the rubber tubing to the same length as the rope.

5 To finish off, pick up a 15º, an 11º seed bead, and a 15º, and sew through the second and third 15ºs, and the open hole of the second twin from the previous round **(photo c)**. Repeat once. Pick up a 15º, an 11º, and a 15º, and sew through the two 15ºs as usual and the same twin as the last stitch of

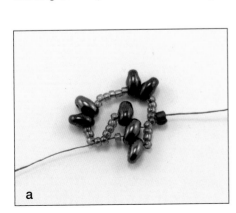

a

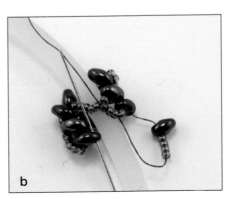

b

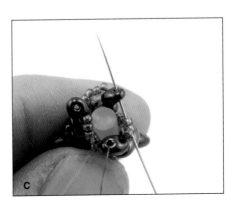

c

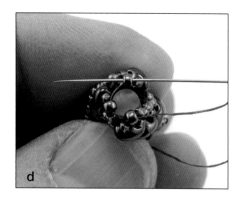

the regular round. Retrace the thread path through the beads to exit the first 11º added in this round.

6 Sew through the next two 11ºs added in the previous round, and then sew through all three beads again, pulling the beads into a snug triangle **(photo d)**.

7 Pick up a bead cap from the wide end, five 11ºs, and sew down through the bead cap again and into the next

11º of the triangle. Do not pull tight. Retrace the thread path through the bead cap, the ring of five 11ºs, **(photo e)** and back through the bead cap, into the third 11º of the triangle. Pull the thread snug. Retrace the thread path through the bead cap, five 11ºs, and bead cap again, and sew from the first 11º in the triangle. Sew into the rope, tying several overhand knots along the way. Trim the thread.

8 To finish the tail-end, remove the stop bead and attach a

needle to the tail. Sew through the second hole of the nearest twin. Pick up a 15º, an 11º, and a 15º, and sew through the first and second 15ºs in the round below, plus the open hole of the available twin in the next pair. Repeat once. Pick up a 15º, an 11º, and a 15º. Sew through the first and second 15ºs, and the same half of the twin stitched through at the beginning of this step. Retrace the thread path through the beads to exit the first 11º added in this round.

9 Work as in steps 6 and 7.

10 Using two pairs of pliers, open one of the jump rings, and attach through the loop of five 11ºs on the end of the rope and the bar end of the toggle clasp. Close the jump ring. Repeat for the other end of the rope using the second jump ring and the other half of the clasp.

Net Results

African tube and loop necklaces were my inspiration for this piece. My version includes a funky cube pendant. The technique is easy and results in a wonderfully supple necklace.

designed by
Susan Yvette England

materials

necklace 27 in. (69cm)

- 11º seed beads:
  30 g color A
  10 g color B
  20 g color C
- clasp
- ½–⅝-in. (1.3–1.6cm) cube wooden block
- nylon beading thread, conditioned with beeswax or Thread Heaven; or Fireline 8 lb. test
- beading needles, #10 or #11

Netted Tube

The tube is composed of seven netting sections separated by loops.

1 On 2 yd. (1.8m) of conditioned thread, pick up a repeating pattern of two color A and one color B 11º seed beads three times. Sew through all the beads again, and, leaving an 8-in. (20cm) tail, tie the beads into a ring.

2 Work in five-bead netting as follows: Pick up two As, one B, and two As, and sew through the next B on the previous round **(fig., a–b)**. Repeat twice to complete the round **(b–c)**. Step up through the first three beads picked up in this round to get into position to begin the next round **(c–d)**.

3 Repeat step 2 16 times.

4 To work the first section of loops, pick up 19 11ºs. My loops are made up of 19 Bs, but pick up a pattern if you like, such as nine As and 10 Bs. Sew through the next B on the previous round **(photo a)**. Repeat twice to complete the round. Step up through the first 10 beads picked up in the first stitch.

5 To begin the second section of netting, pick up two As, one B, and two As, and sew through the middle 11º of the next loop on the previous round **(photo b)**. Repeat twice to complete the round, and step up through the first three beads picked up in this round.

6 Repeat step 2 19 times.

7 To work the second section of loops, repeat step 4 with the

same combination of beads, or a new combination.

8 To begin the third section of netting, work as in step 5, but pick up two color C 11ºs, one B, and two Cs, and sew through the middle 11º of the next loop on the previous round. For the next 23 rounds, continue in five-bead netting, picking up two Cs, one B, and two Cs for each stitch and sewing through the next B on the previous round.

9 To work the third section of loops, repeat step 4.

10 For the middle section of netting, work as in step 5, with the following changes: For round 1, pick up two Bs, one A, and two Bs for each stitch, and sew through the middle 11º of the next loop on the previous

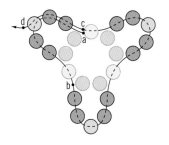

FIG.

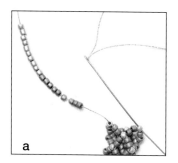

a

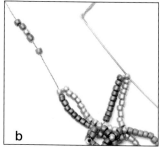

b

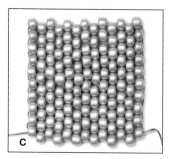

c

NOTE: With nylon beading thread, the netting will be flexible and will flatten out somewhat. For better shape, try stitching with Fireline.

round. For round 2, pick up two Bs, one C, and two Bs, and sew through the next A on the previous round. Continue working this section of netting, using Bs as the primary color and alternating between using an A for the middle bead of each stitch on one round and a C for the middle bead of each stitch on the next round. Work a total of 16 rounds.

11 Make the next three sections each of loops and netting by following steps 2–9 in reverse order.

12 For the final round, pick up two As, and sew through the next B on the previous round. Repeat twice, sew through all nine beads of the last row, and tie a half-hitch knot.

13 Sew through two beads on the final round, and pick up half of a clasp. Skip three beads on the final round, sew through the next three beads, and sew back through the clasp. Repeat, secure the tail with a few half-hitch knots, and trim. Repeat on the other end of the tube, using the 8-in. (20cm) tail.

Cube Pendant

1 On 2 ft. (61cm) of conditioned thread, pick up a stop bead and 10 Bs. Continuing in color B, work approximately 18 rows of flat, even-count peyote stitch. Change the number of rows and the number of beads across each row if needed to fit around your core block and to keep the panel square **(photo c)**. Do not tie off the tails. Set aside. Make a second color B square panel.

2 On 1 yd. (.9m) of thread, work a panel in color A that is the same size as the color B panels. Working a continuous strip of four panels, stitch a panel in color C, another panel in color A, and another panel in color C **(photo d)**. Zip up the end panels **(photo e)** to form a tube.

3 Sew one B panel to an open side of the tube, and sew one edge of the other B panel to the remaining open side.

4 Slip the core bead into the beadwork, and sew the remaining seams closed **(photo f)**.

5 Exiting one corner of the cube, pick up six 11°s, and sew through an adjacent corner bead **(photo g)**. Repeat to

make loops along the length of all the seams.

6 Sew through the beadwork to exit the corner you wish to have as the top of your pendant. Pick up approximately 30 Bs, and sew through an adjacent bead on the cube. Retrace the thread path several times, secure the tails with a few half-hitch knots, and trim. Slide the loop of the pendant onto the netted tube.

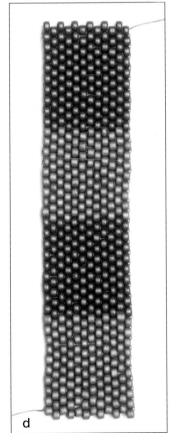

d

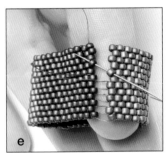

e

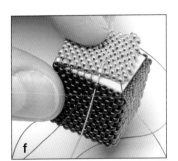

f

g

NOTE: Measure your beadwork against the core cube frequently as you stitch to make sure the beadwork will cover the form completely.

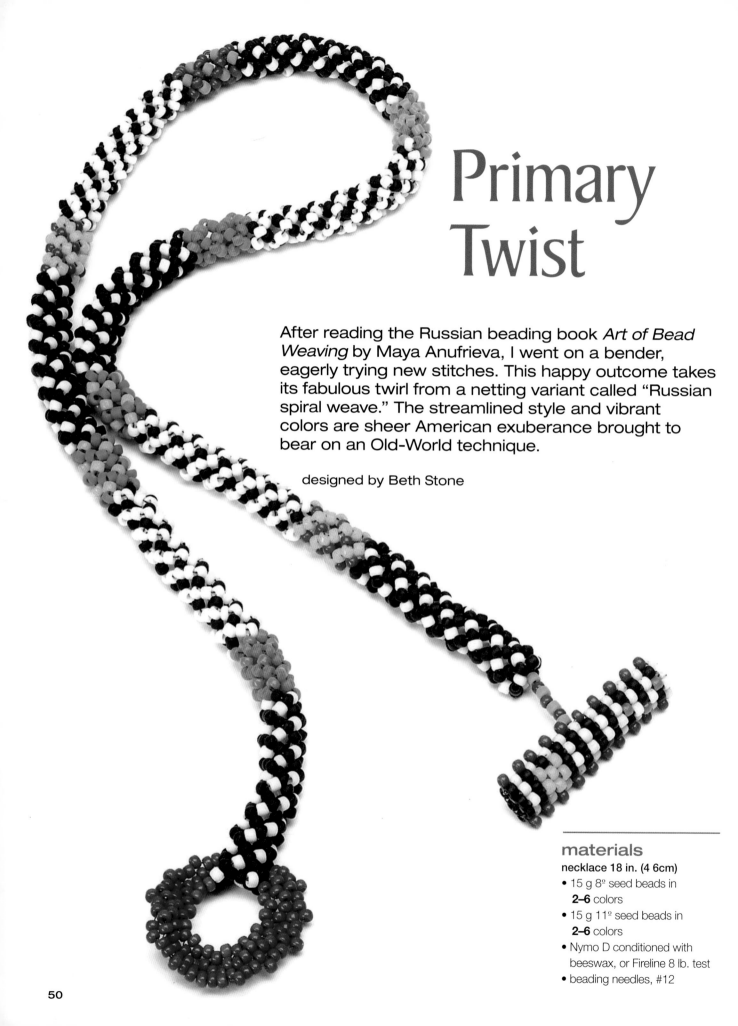

Primary
Twist

After reading the Russian beading book *Art of Bead Weaving* by Maya Anufrieva, I went on a bender, eagerly trying new stitches. This happy outcome takes its fabulous twirl from a netting variant called "Russian spiral weave." The streamlined style and vibrant colors are sheer American exuberance brought to bear on an Old-World technique.

designed by Beth Stone

materials

necklace 18 in. (4 6cm)

- 15 g 8º seed beads in **2–6** colors
- 15 g 11º seed beads in **2–6** colors
- Nymo D conditioned with beeswax, or Fireline 8 lb. test
- beading needles, #12

Netted Tube

1 Start a 3-yd (2.7m) length of thread and pick up two 11º seed beads and one 8º seed bead three times, for a total of nine beads.

2 Leaving a 1-yd. (.9m) tail, sew through all beads again in the same direction to form a ring. Exit the first 11º **(fig. 1, a-b)**.

3 Pick up an 8º and two 11ºs. Sew through the 11º after the next 8º on the ring **(fig. 2, a–b)**. Repeat around the ring **(b–c)**. Step up through the first 8º and 11º **(c–d)**.

4 Repeat step 3 until you reach the desired length.

5 To close the tube, stitch the last round, picking up an 8º instead of an 8º and two 11ºs. Sew through the three 8ºs just added a few times and cinch the tube closed **(photo a)**. Secure the working thread with half-hitch knots between a few beads. Don't trim the thread. Set aside.

Clasp

1 Thread a needle on the long tail and pick up 24 11ºs. Sew into a bead on the opposite side of the netted tube to form a ring **(photo b** and **fig. 3, a–b)**.

2 Sew around the tube, following the thread path of the netting, and exit the bead below point a **(b–c)**. Work one round of peyote over the new beads **(c–d)**. Sew through the tube as before **(d–e)**. Increase to two-drop peyote in the fourth round.

3 Continue alternating a row of single-bead peyote with a row of two-drop until the ring is the desired size (six to eight rounds). Secure the thread in the bead-work and trim.

4 To make the toggle end of the clasp, start a 1-yd. length of thread. Pick up 20 11ºs and work flat, even-count peyote for 12 rows.

5 Fold the peyote strip so the first and last row of beads are aligned. Zip up the two ends to form a tube.

a

b

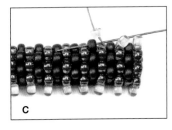

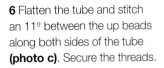

c

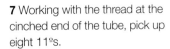

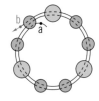

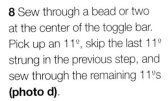

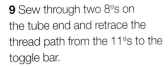

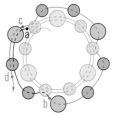

d

6 Flatten the tube and stitch an 11º between the up beads along both sides of the tube **(photo c)**. Secure the threads.

7 Working with the thread at the cinched end of the tube, pick up eight 11ºs.

8 Sew through a bead or two at the center of the toggle bar. Pick up an 11º, skip the last 11º strung in the previous step, and sew through the remaining 11ºs **(photo d)**.

9 Sew through two 8ºs on the tube end and retrace the thread path from the 11ºs to the toggle bar.

10 Reinforce the thread path a few more times, sewing through different 8º pairs on the end of the tube each time. Secure the thread and trim.

FIG. 1

FIG. 2

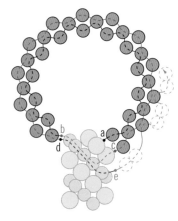

Color play For the necklace on the left, I changed bead colors every 1½ in. (3.8cm). For the necklace on p. 50, I alternated 1½ in. of black and white seed beads with ¼ in. (6mm) of various colors.

FIG. 3

Dancing Dangles

The distinct lines of this V-shaped
necklace remind me of the fashions of
the Roaring Twenties. Enhanced with
a bit of fringe and fire-polished beads,
this necklace would have looked great
on Zelda Fitzgerald as she danced the
Charleston. This adaptation of traditional
St. Petersburg chain lets you add
dangles to a simple V-line necklace.

designed by Mary DiMatteo

As you stitch the chain, pull the new beads tight to the previous stitch.

1 On a length of thread, attach a stop bead, leaving an 8-in. (20cm) tail. Pick up seven cube beads, and sew through the fourth and fifth beads again, pulling the sixth and seventh beads beside them to form two columns **(fig. 1, a–b)**. Pick up a 4mm fire-polished bead and a 15º seed bead, and sew back through the 4mm and the next three cubes **(b–c)**. Pick up a cube, and sew through the two cubes in the next column **(c–d)**.

2 Pick up four cubes, and sew through the first two cubes again **(fig. 2, a–b)**. Pick up a 4mm and a 15º and sew back through the 4mm and all the cubes in the column **(b–c)**. Pick up a 15º and sew through the first two cubes in the column **(c–d)**. Pick up a cube, and sew down through the cubes in the next column **(d–e)**.

3 Repeat step 2 until the chain is 8 in. long. Make a second chain identical to the first.

4 Exit the bottom cube in the last column of a chain **(fig. 3, a)**.

Pick up three cubes, and sew through the third cube in the previous column and the first cube picked up **(a–b)** to make a new two-bead column. Pick up a 15º and sew back through all the cubes in the column **(b–c)**.

5 Pick up a 15º and sew back through the top bead in the column **(c–d)**. Pick up a cube, and sew down through the two beads in the next column. Pick up 10 cubes, a 4mm, and a 15º **(d–e)**. Skip the 15º and sew back through all the beads in the column **(e–f)**.

materials

necklace 17 in. (43cm)

- **99** 4mm fire-polished beads
- 7 g 1.5mm cube beads
- 2.5 g 15º seed beads
- clasp with optional extension chain
- Fireline 6 lb. test or nylon beading thread, size D
- beading needles, #12

NOTE: Narrower fire-polished beads give the necklace a more fluid drape, while wider beads give the chain a fuller look and enhance the curve.

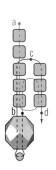

FIG. 1

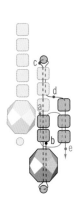

FIG. 2

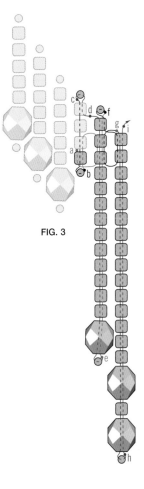

FIG. 3

6 Pick up a 15º and sew through the top cube in the column. Pick up two cubes, and sew up through the third and second cubes in the previous column **(f–g)**. Sew through the two new cubes again, and pick up 13 cubes, a 4mm, a cube, a 4mm, and a 15º **(g–h)**. Skip the 15º and sew back through all the beads in the column **(h–i)**. Set this half aside.

7 Repeat steps 4 and 5 on the other chain **(fig. 4, a–b)**. Pick up a 15º and sew back through the top cube in the column **(b–c)**.

8 Place the two chains side by side, so they meet in the center. Using the thread from step 7, sew down through the first two beads in the center column **(c–d)**. Sew up through the adjacent two beads in the next column **(d–e)**. Weave the thread into the beadwork, secure with a few half-hitch knots, and trim.

9 The remaining thread should be exiting the top cube of the center column **(point f)**. Pick up a 15º and sew back through the top two cubes in the column **(f–g)**. Sew through the two adjacent beads in the next column on the other chain **(g–h)**. Secure the thread in the beadwork, and trim.

10 On one end of the necklace, remove the stop bead, and thread a needle on the tail. Sew through the fourth and third cubes from the end, so that the first and second cubes form a new column **(fig. 5, a–b)**. Pick up three 15º, half of the clasp, and three 15º, and sew through the new column again **(b–c)**. Pick up a 15º and sew back through the two cubes, six 15º, and the next two cubes **(c–d)**. Retrace the thread path a few times, secure the tail in the beadwork, and trim.

11 Repeat step 10 on the other end of the necklace. If desired, an extension chain can be used for the second half of the clasp.

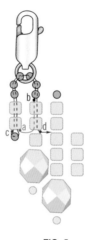

FIG. 5

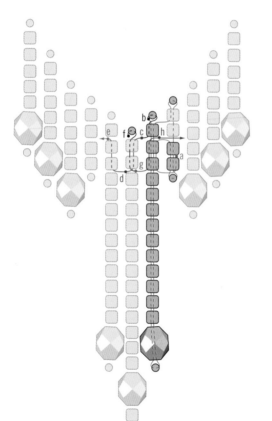

FIG. 4

Russian Wraparound

Russian spiral takes netting on a roller coaster ride, producing a flexible corkscrew rope perfect for a necklace or bracelet. Use some unexpected elements for the core, like a macramé ring or vinyl tubing.

designed by Carolyn Cave

materials

blue bangle 2½ in. (6.4cm) inside diameter

- 5 g 6mm bugle beads (teal)
- 3 g 11º seed beads in each of **3** colors: A (dark blue), B (sky blue), C (blue-green)
- 5 g 15º seed beads (Miyuki 332, fancy forest green)
- 3-in. (7.6cm) macramé ring
- Fireline 6 lb. test
- beading needles, #10 and #12
- bias seam binding (optional)
- sewing thread (to match binding, optional)
- sewing needle (optional)

red necklace 18–20 in. (46–51cm)

- 10 g 6mm bugle beads (red)
- **2** 3mm bugle beads (red)
- 5 g 11º seed beads in each of **3** colors: A (ruby), B (amethyst), C (raspberry)
- 7 g 15º seed beads (Miyuki 298, transparent rainbow burgundy)

clasp

- **2** 7–9mm diameter cones or bead caps
- 4mm vinyl tubing
- Fireline 6 lb. test
- beading needles, #10 and #12

pink bracelet colors:

- 6mm bugle beads (Miyuki BGL2-001, silver-lined crystal)
- 3mm bugle beads (Miyuki BGL1-001, silver-lined crystal)
- 11º seed beads color A (Miyuki 11-596, opaque tearose luster) color B (Miyuki 11-1, silver-lined crystal) color C (Miyuki 11-155 F, matte transparent pale pink)
- 15º seed beads (Toho 15R741, copper-lined alabaster)

Bangle

1 If desired, wrap bias seam binding around the macramé ring to make the ring 4mm thick all the way around. Overlap the ends of the binding slightly, then trim the excess. Using a sewing needle and thread, sew the ends of the binding together.

2 On a length of Fireline, pick up three 15º seed beads, a 6mm bugle bead, three 15ºs, a color A 11º seed bead, three 15ºs, a color B 11º seed bead, three 15ºs, a color C 11º seed bead, and two 15ºs, leaving a 6-in. (15cm) tail. Tie the beads into a ring around the macramé ring with a square knot. Sew through the first 15º again.

3 Pick up a bugle and two 15ºs, and sew through the first 15º after the bugle in the previous round **(fig., a–b)**. Pick up an A and two 15ºs, and sew through the first 15º after the A in the previous round **(b–c)**. Pick up a B and two 15ºs, and sew through the first 15º after the B in the previous round **(c–d)**. Pick up a C and two 15ºs, and sew through the first 15º after the C in the previous round **(d–e)**.

4 Continue as in step 3 **(e–f)** to form the spiral rope around the macramé ring, ending and adding thread as needed. Stop when there is 3–4mm between the ends of the spiral rope, ending with a C stitch.

5 Twist the spiral rope as necessary so the bead pattern on the ends line up.

6 To begin connecting the ends, pick up a bugle, and sew through the 15º just before the A in the first round **(photo a)**. Pick up a 15º and sew through the 15º just after the bugle added in the last round **(photo b)**.

7 Pick up an A, and sew through the 15º just before the B in the first round **(photo c)**. Pick up a 15º and sew through the 15º just after the A in the last round **(photo d)**. The thread should form a zigzag between the two ends.

8 Pick up a B, and sew through the 15º just before the C in the first round. Pick up a 15º and sew through the 15º just after the B in the last round.

9 Pick up a C, and sew through the 15º just before the bugle in the first round. Pick up a 15º and sew through the 15º just after the C in the last round.

10 Sew through the next bugle and 15º, and retrace the thread path through the connecting round. End the working thread and tail.

NOTE: In the blue bangle, the bugle beads are 2mm in diameter and the seed beads are Czech 11ºs. In the pink version, the bugle beads are 1.5mm in diameter and the seed beads are Japanese 11ºs, which are thicker. The result: The blue bangle has smaller gaps between the bugles, though gaps will not detract from the overall look of the piece.

▭	6 mm bugle bead
●	11º seed bead, color A
●	11º seed bead, color B
○	11º seed bead, color C
●	15º seed bead

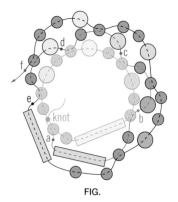

FIG.

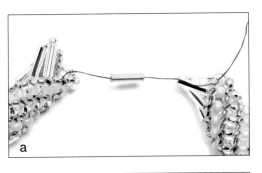

a

b

c

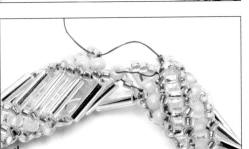

d

e

Necklace

1 Determine the desired finished length of your necklace, and subtract the length of the clasp and each cone or bead cap. Cut a piece of vinyl tubing to that length.

2 Work step 2 of "Bangle," but leave a 10-in. (25cm) tail, and tie the beads around one end of the vinyl tubing.

3 Work step 3 of "Bangle," and repeat for the length of the tubing, ending and adding thread as needed. End with a bugle stitch.

4 Pick up a color A 11º seed bead and a 15º seed bead, and sew through the first 15º after the A in the previous round. Pick up a B and a 15º and sew through the first 15º after the B in the previous round. Pick up a C and a 15º and sew through the first 15º after the C in the previous round. Pick up a 3mm bugle bead and a 15º and sew through the 15º after the 6mm bugle in the previous round.

5 Sew through the new A, B, C, and 15º after the 3mm bugle, pulling tight to taper the end of the rope. Sew through the beads again, exiting the 15º.

6 Pick up a cone or bead cap, nine 15ºs, and half of the clasp. Sew back through the first 15º picked up and the cone or bead cap, and sew through the top A on the tapered end **(photo e)**. Retrace the thread path through the clasp connection, and sew through the top B on the tapered end. Retrace the thread path once more, and sew through the top C on the tapered end. End the working thread.

7 Repeat steps 4–6 on the other end of the necklace, keeping in mind that you will be stitching the last round in the opposite direction and picking up 11ºs in reverse order.

Daisy Vine

Offset crystals nestled within rings of seed beads
resemble a twining vine of daisies in this charming
necklace. Make a shorter length for a matching bracelet.
Different sized seed beads provide textural contrast in
the loops that encircle the bicone crystals.

designed by Karen Price

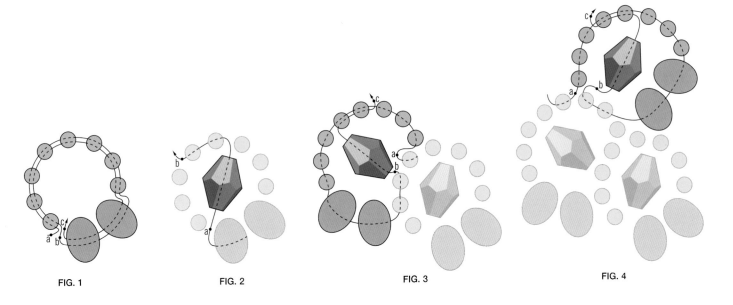

FIG. 1   FIG. 2   FIG. 3   FIG. 4

Necklace

1 On 2 ft. (61cm) of conditioned thread, leave a 10-in. (25cm) tail, and pick up eight 11º seed beads and two 6º seed beads **(fig. 1, a–b)**. Sew through the beads to form a ring **(b–c)**, and tie a surgeon's knot.

2 Pick up a crystal, and sew through the fifth and then the fourth 11º of the ring **(fig. 2, a–b)**.

3 Pick up eight 11ºs and two 6ºs, and sew through the second and third 11ºs of the previous ring **(fig. 3, a–b)**.

4 Pick up a crystal and sew through the fifth and then the fourth 11º just added **(b–c)**.

5 Repeat steps 3 **(fig. 4, a–b)** and 4 **(b–c)** until your necklace is ½ in. (1.3cm) short of the desired length. Add thread as needed.

6 Secure the tail with a few half-hitch knots between beads, and trim.

Toggle Bar and Loop

1 To make the beaded toggle bar, pick up 10 11ºs and stitch eight rows in flat, even-count peyote. You will have a strip 10 beads wide, with four beads along each straight edge. Zip up the strip to form a tube.

2 Retrace the thread path to reinforce the join. Exit an end 11º.

3 Pick up an 11º, a 6º, and an 11º. Sew back through the tube beadwork to the other end.

4 Repeat step 3, but after adding the end beads, sew into the tube and exit at the center of the bar between two beads.

5 To attach the tube to the necklace, pick up three 11ºs and sew counterclockwise through the last ring of the necklace to anchor the thread. Sew back through the three 11ºs picked up in this step, the toggle bar, and the three 11ºs. Secure the thread in the ring with a few half-hitch knots, and trim.

6 To add the loop for the toggle bar, thread a needle on the tail and pick up enough 11ºs (approximately 24) to fit around the toggle bar. Sew back through the first two 11ºs just added, make a half-hitch knot, and retrace the thread path to reinforce the loop. Secure the thread with a few half-hitch knots, and trim.

materials

necklace 15 in. (38cm)

- **62** 4mm bicone crystals
- 9 g 6º seed beads
- 5 g 11º seed beads
- Nymo D, conditioned with beeswax or Thread Heaven
- beading needles, #12

NOTE: A beaded toggle bar closure gives visual continuity to the necklace.

Side by Side

This necklace is based on a stitch that I learned from a friendly shopkeeper in Ephesus, Turkey. The stitch, known in Turkey by names such as Snakes Bones or Railway, is normally done with small beads and fine thread and used to trim textiles. It lends itself to experimentation and looks entirely different when made with larger beads. Work this stitch side to side—you don't have to guess at length. Add an eye-catching clasp to finish.

designed by Adele Rogers Recklies

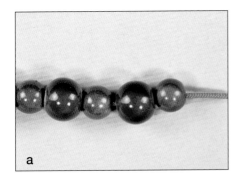

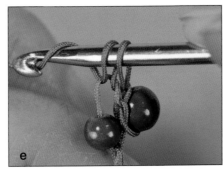

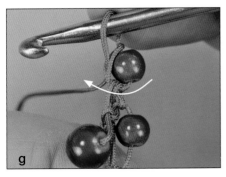

materials

necklace 22 in. (56cm)

- **48** 8mm acrylic beads
- **48** 6mm acrylic beads
- 9 yds. Glisten novelty knitting yarn
- 8½ in. (21.6cm) 20-gauge, silver-colored craft wire
- 4 in. (10cm) 22-gauge, silver-colored craft wire
- ceramic clasp (Sarah Lee Rhoads)
- **20** 5mm silver-colored jump rings
- size F (3.75mm) crochet hook
- wire cutters
- roundnose pliers
- chainnose pliers
- needlenose pliers
- size 18 tapestry needle

Necklace

Gauge: six beads crocheted into three pairs=1¼ in. (3.2cm)

String the Necklace

String an 8mm bead and 16mm bead 48 times **(photo a)** for a crochet piece that measures approximately 21 in. (53cm) minus the clasp. See p. 64 for tips on stringing beads onto yarn.

Crochet the Necklace
Set Up Rows

1 Leaving a 5-in.(13cm) tail, make a slip knot and work a chain stitch. Slide down a 6mm bead and work a chain stitch over the bead **(photo b)**.

2 Slide the 8mm bead down and work a chain stitch over the next bead **(photo c)**.

3 Twist the top (8mm) bead 180 degrees horizontally to get to the 6mm bead and make a single crochet in the thread holding that bead **(photos d, e)**. Notice the two beads are now almost side by side.

Main Crochet

1 Slide down the next 6mm bead and work a chain stitch over the bead **(photo f)**.

2 Turn the work 180 degrees **(photo g)**, insert the hook in the loop holding the 8mm bead previously crocheted **(photo h)** and make a single crochet. Repeat steps 1 and 2 until necklace is approximately 21 in. or the desired length. An example of three repeats of the crochet stitch can be seen in **photo i**.

3 Leaving a 5-in. tail, cut thread, and fasten off.

Wire Connectors
Make Wire Connectors

1 Cut a 4¼-in. (10.8cm) piece of 20-gauge wire. Fold it gently

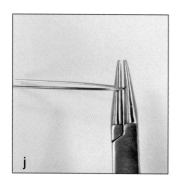

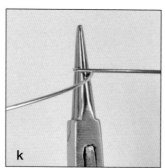

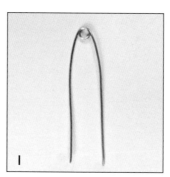

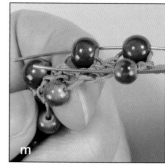

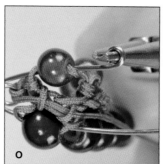

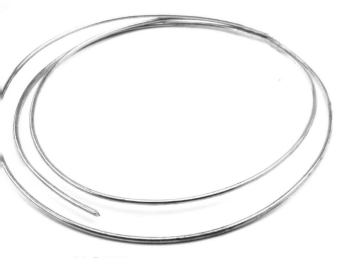

NOTE Use silver-colored wire. Photos use colored wire for visibility. If you don't want the wire support to show, wrap each side with the remaining thread tail before you weave in the end.

in half and place the fold in the chainnose pliers, ⅜–½ in.(1–1.3cm) below tip of the pliers with the fold facing you **(photo j)**.

2 Bend the left wire to the right, around the pliers and away from you. Bend the right wire to the left around the pliers and away from you **(photo k)**. You now have a U-shaped piece of wire with a double loop at one end **(photo l)**. Squeeze the loops closer together if they are separated. Make another wire connector.

Attach Connectors to the Crochet

1 Place the ends of a wire connector through the first beads of the necklace. Pull the connector down until the double

loop reaches the end of the crocheted thread **(photo m)**.

2 Thread a needle on the tail and sew through the double loop of the wire support and the necklace two times **(photo n)**. Make a knot and weave in the end.

3 With wire cutters, trim the wire end sticking out of each bead to ½ in. (1.3cm) Using roundnose and chainnose pliers, make a spiral on each wire end **(photos o, p)**.

4 Repeat steps 1–3 on the other end of the crocheted rope.

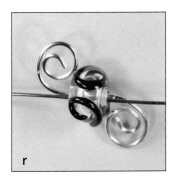

r

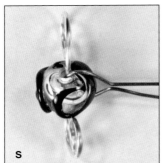

s

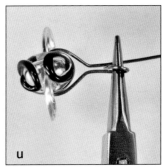

t

u

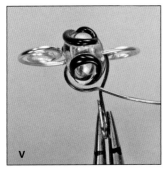

v

w

x

Clasp
Attach Connector to Ceramic Clasp

1 Open the jump ring.

2 Attach the double loop of the wire connector and the wire loop of the ceramic clasp. Close the jump ring **(photo q)**.

Make Wire Loop on the Glass Bead

1 Cut a 4-in. (10cm) piece of 22-gauge wire. String the wire through the glass bead leaving a 1¼-in. (3.2cm) tail **(photo r)**.

2 Bend both sides of wire to make a triangle, about ⅛ in. (3mm) below the bead **(photo s)**.

3 Grasp the shorter wire with the roundnose pliers ⅜ in. (1cm)below the glass bead **(photo t)** and make a

loop around the pliers **(photo u)**. Trim the wire to ⅛–¼ in. Squeeze the wires together.

4 Make a 90-degree bend in the long end of the wire **(photo v)** Wrap the long wire around the short wire down to the loop at the bottom **(photo w)**. Trim the excess wire.

Fasten Glass Bead to the Crochet

1 Open the jump ring.

2 Attach the double loop of the wire connector and the wire loop at the bottom of the glass bead. Close the jump ring **(photo x)**.

Hints For Stringing Beads On Cord

Stringing beads on cord or knitting yarn may take a bit of ingenuity because the yarn end is bulky and it tends to fray. One solution is to dip the end of the yarn in glue, form it into a point, and use that as a needle. Another method uses a needle to string the beads:

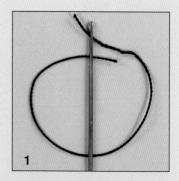

- On about 3 in. (7.6cm) of thread, attach a needle from right to left.

- Thread the other end of the 3-in. thread through the eye of the needle from left to right **(photo 1)**.

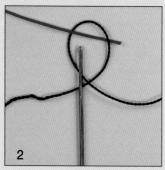

- Pull the two ends of the thread to form a small loop.

- Place your yarn through the thread loop **(photo 2)**, leaving a tail of at least 2 in. (5cm).

- Pull the thread loop tight against the yarn, and gather all of the tails together.

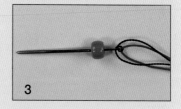

- Pick up a bead with the needle **(photo 3)**, and slide the bead over the thread and the yarn **(photo 4)**.

- If your yarn unravels easily, apply glue on the unraveled yarns and form them into a point.

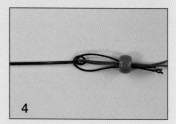

- You might also be able to take those unraveled yarns and put them through the thread loop on your needle (as above), for a thinner "yarn" to get your beads over.

- If you have a yarn with "eyelashes" or squares of fibers between two yarns, cut off the extra fibers on the beginning 2–3 in. to make a thinner "yarn" to get the beads over.

- If the beads are plastic, use a diamond bead reamer to make the bead hole a little larger.

Turkish Delight

While the origin of this variation of bead crochet is unclear, Adele Rogers Recklies calls it Turkish Loops. The technique, also known as perlen crochet or jewelry crochet, has appeared in Japan, Germany, and Austria, among other places. It is easy to learn for beginners. Try the two-loop bracelet first to practice and then move on to the three-loop bracelet and the necklace.

bracelets designed by Adele Rogers Recklies
necklace designed by Keiko Seki

materials

all projects
- beading cord, size E or F or equivalent
- twisted-wire or Big Eye needle
- beading needles, #10
- 1.5mm crochet hook
- paper clip or safety pin

two-loop bracelet 7 in. (18cm)
- **41** 4mm fire-polished beads in each of **2** colors: A, B
- 5 g 11º seed beads
- button with shank
- **2** 6–8mm bead caps

three-loop bracelet 7 in.
- **111** 4mm fire-polished beads
- 5 g 11º seed beads
- button with shank
- **2** 9–10mm bead caps

necklace 17 in. (43cm)
plus 2 ½-in. (6.4cm)
- dangle
- 20x12mm glass or gemstone focal bead
- **7** 6–12mm fire-polished beads
- **5** 64mm faux pearls, color A
- **5** 56mm bugle beads in each of **3** colors: A, B, C
- 11º seed beads
  3 g color A
  5 g in each of **2** colors: B, C
- **10** 5–8mm spacers
- toggle clasp
- nylon or GSP beading thread, size D or 6 lb. test

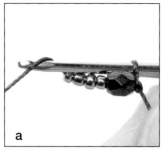

a

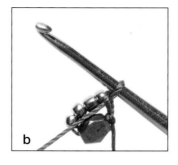

b

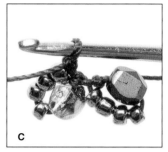

c

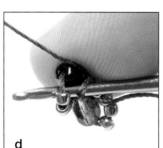

d

e

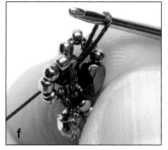

f

Two-loop bracelet

1 With a twisted-wire or Big Eye needle attached to the end of the cord, string a repeating pattern of four 11º seed beads, a color A 4mm fire-polished bead, four 11ºs, and a color B 4mm fire-polished bead 41 times. Make a slip knot approximately 8 in. (20cm) from the end of the cord. Insert the hook into the slip knot.

2 Slide the first group of one 4mm and four 11ºs down to the knot, and, with the hook, grasp the cord right after the fourth 11º **(photo a)**. Pull the cord through the loop on the hook to work a chain stitch **(photo b)**. Grasp the cord with the hook, and pull it through the loop on the hook to work another chain stitch without beads.

3 Repeat step 2 **(photo c)**. You have now completed the stitches for round 1, which consists of two beaded loops. It will be pulled into a tubular form in the next round.

4 Insert the hook in the middle of the first loop in the previous round, between the 4mm and the first 11º. Make sure the 4mm is behind the hook and the 11ºs are in front **(photo d)**. Slide the next group of beads up to the previous stitch. The 4mm in the new stitch should be the same color as the 4mm in the stitch into which you inserted your hook. With the hook, grasp the cord after the fourth 11º **(photo e)**, and pull it through the loop on the hook to work a slip stitch **(photo f)**. Grasp the cord again, and pull it through the loop on the hook to work a slip stitch without beads between the two groups of 11ºs. Repeat in the second loop of the previous round.

5 Work as in step 4 until the rope is about 1½ in. (3.8cm) short of the desired length. Place a paper clip or safety pin in the last stitch to temporarily hold your place.

6 Attach a beading needle to the tail, and string a bead cap, three or four 11ºs, the button, and three or four 11ºs.

7 Sew back through the bead cap, and into the crochet stitches at the end of the bracelet **(photo g)**. Sew around the cord in the core of the bracelet, and retrace the thread path through the bead cap, the 11ºs, and the button, exiting through the core of the bracelet. Tie a half-hitch knot, weave the tail through the bracelet core a few times, and trim.

8 Remove the paper clip or safety pin, and continue working in two-loop crochet until the rope is the desired length or you've used all the beads. Work one more round without beads to close up the end. Leaving a 12-in. (30cm) tail, trim the cord, and pull it through the last stitch.

9 Attach a beading needle, and string a bead cap and enough 11ºs to make a loop around the button. Sew back through the bead cap, and continue into the crochet stitches at the end of the bracelet. Secure and end the cord as in step 7.

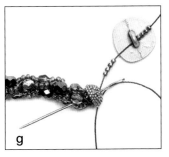

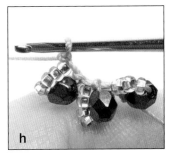

Style Option
Dangle the drop in front for a Y-necklace, or wear it in back for a classic round neckline.

Three-loop Bracelet

Work as in the two-loop bracelet, with the following changes:

Begin by stringing a repeating pattern of four 11º seed beads and a 4mm 111 times.

Make round 1 with three loops instead of two **(photo h).**

Work three sets of stitches per round.

Subtle Shades
A monochromatic color palette suits this design well, enhancing the elegant lines and spiraling pattern.

Necklace

1 String the following sequence a total of five times: a color A 6mm bugle bead, two color A 11º seed beads, a 4mm pearl, a color B 6mm bugle bead, four color B 11º seed beads, a color C 6mm bugle bead, and four color C 11º seed beads. Make a slip knot 12 in. (30cm) from the end of the cord, and insert the hook into the slip knot.

2 To work the first round, slide the first group of color C beads up to the slip knot, and work a chain stitch. Work another chain stitch without any beads. Slide the group of color B beads up, and work two chain stitches. Slide the group of color A beads up, and work two chain stitches.

3 Work in three-loop crochet as in the bracelet, inserting the hook after the bugle in each stitch. Continue until you've stitched all the beads. Work three more stitches without beads to tighten up the end, trim the cord to 8 in. (20cm), and pull the tail through the last stitch.

4 Attach a beading needle to the 12-in. (30cm) tail, and pick up an alternating sequence of fire-polished beads and spacers to equal about 2½–3 in. (6.4–7.6cm). Pick up five 11ºs in your choice of color, the loop half of the toggle clasp, and five 11ºs, and sew back through the beads just added and into the core of the crochet rope **(photo i)**. Retrace the thread path through all the beads and the clasp. End the cord within the rope, as in step 7 of "Two-loop bracelet."

5 Attach a beading needle to the other end, and pick up a spacer, five 11ºs, the bar half of the clasp, and five 11ºs. Sew back through the spacer, and continue into the end of the crochet rope. Retrace the thread path, and end the cord.

6 To add the dangle, on 18 in. (46cm) of beading thread, pick up a 4mm pearl, a spacer bead, a 6mm fire-polished bead, a spacer, a 10mm fire-polished bead, a spacer, the 20x12mm bead, and three seed beads. Skip the seed beads, and sew back through the rest of the beads added in this step.

7 Pick up 10 11ºs and the toggle loop, and retrace the thread path through the dangle beads. Sew back through them again so both the working thread and the tail are coming out between the same beads, and tie a square knot. End the threads.

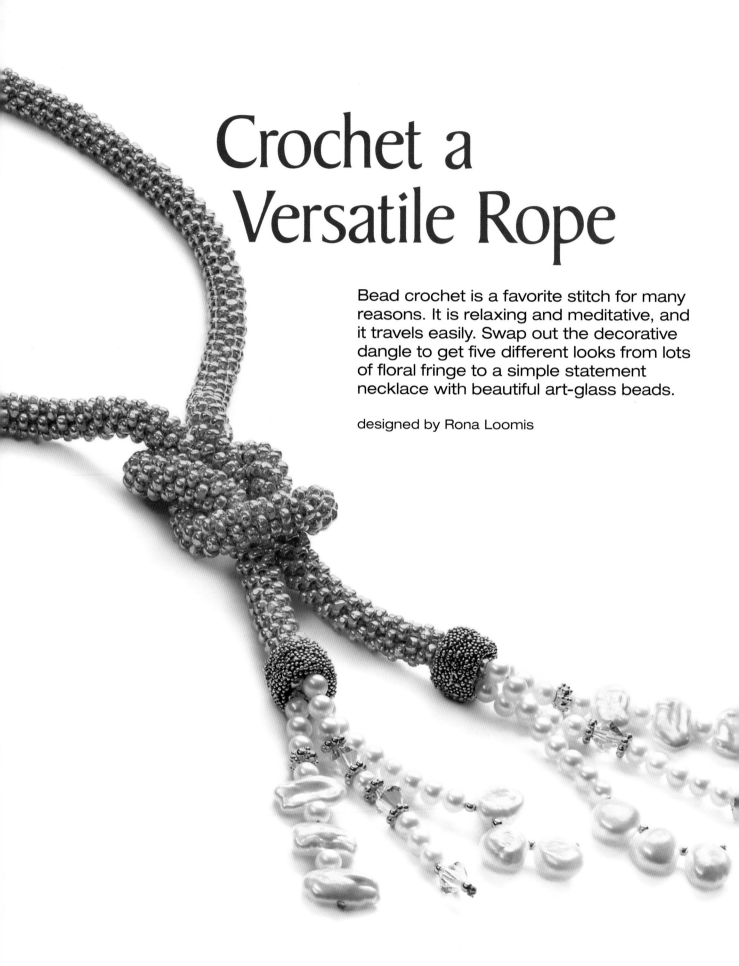

Crochet a Versatile Rope

Bead crochet is a favorite stitch for many reasons. It is relaxing and meditative, and it travels easily. Swap out the decorative dangle to get five different looks from lots of floral fringe to a simple statement necklace with beautiful art-glass beads.

designed by Rona Loomis

Crocheted Rope

The base of this necklace is a 16–18 in. (41–46cm) crocheted rope. My base rope is worked using four 8º seed beads per round, approximately 48 8ºs per in. (2.5cm). When determining your desired length, keep in mind the fringed centerpiece rope will take up about 2 in. (5cm) of the base row's length when it is knotted to the base.

1 String enough 8ºs on silk thread to make your base rope the desired length. Leaving an 8-in. (20cm) tail, work in single crochet. After you complete the last round, work one row of chain stitches, and pull the working thread through the last stitch, leaving an 8-in. tail.

2 Thread a needle on one tail. Sew into the center of the base rope, a few inches away from the end. Tie several half-hitch knots between the beads, and trim. Repeat with the other tail.

3 Secure 1 yd. (.9m) of Fireline in the base, and exit the center of the rope on one end. Pick up a bead cap, a 3–4mm metal bead, and the soldered jump ring of the S-clasp **(photo a)**. Sew back through the bead and the bead cap. Sew into the center of the rope, and make a few knots. Retrace the thread path twice to reinforce the clasp. Secure the tail as before, and trim. Repeat on the other end with a soldered jump ring.

4 Repeat steps 1–2 to make a 7-in. (18cm) centerpiece rope. Then choose one of the following fringe options to finish the ends.

Embellishments

For the art glass and crystal drop embellishments, secure 1 yd. of Fireline, and exit the center of the centerpiece rope. For the pearl, floral, and grape fringes, secure 3 yd. (2.7m) of Fireline, and exit one of the end 8ºs. Slide the end caps onto the ends of the centerpiece rope. When finished, the embellishments may hold the end caps in place, but if they don't, dot glue on the inside of the end caps after all tails have been secured, slide the end caps into place, and let them dry.

Art Glass (p. 70)

Pick up a bead cap, a 2mm metal bead, a 6mm crystal, an art bead, a 6mm crystal, and a 15º seed bead. Skip the 15º and sew back through the remaining beads and into the rope **(photo b)**. Retrace the thread path two times, and secure the thread as before. Repeat on the other end.

Crystal Drop (p. 70)

Pick up a bead cap, and sew through the top of the crystal. Sew back through the bead cap and into the rope. Reinforce the thread path two times, and secure the thread as before. Repeat on the other end.

Pearl Fringe (p. 68)

1 Pick up a bead cap, sewing through the large opening first. Pick up eight 4mm pearls, a 2mm bead or an 11º seed bead, an 8mm pearl, an 11º, an 8mm, an 11º, an 8mm, and an 11º. Skip the 11º, and sew through the remaining beads and into the rope. Exit the next end 8º.

2 Pick three 4mm pearls, a 4mm spacer, a 6mm crystal, a 4mm spacer, a 4mm pearl, a 4mm spacer, a 6mm crystal, three 4mm pearls, a 2mm bead or 11º, a 6mm crystal, and a 2mm bead. Skip the last bead strung, and sew through the

materials

all projects
- silk thread, size FF
- crochet needle, size #10
- Fireline 6 lb. test
- beading needles, #12

necklace 16–19 in. (41–48cm)
- 30g 8º seed beads
- **2** 3–4mm metal beads (to match clasp)
- **2** 8–10mm bead caps (bottom diameter)
- S-clasp with soldered jump rings

art glass
- **2** 20mm art beads or other beads
- **4** 6mm crystals
- **2** 2mm metal beads or 11º seed beads
- **2** 14º or 15º seed beads
- **2** 6–8mm bead caps
- crystal drop
- **2** 20mm round top-drilled Swarovski crystals
- 15 g 8º seed beads
- **2** 8–10mm end caps (bottom diameter)

pearl fringe
- **2** 6–8mm crystals
- **6** 8mm pearls
- **6** 6mm crystals
- **6** 6mm pearls
- **42** 4mm pearls
- **8** 4mm spacers
- **14** 2mm metal beads
- **2** 8–10mm end caps (bottom diameter)
- glue (optional)

floral fringe
- **60** assorted pressed glass leaves and flower beads
- 5 g 11º seed beads
- **2** 8–10mm end caps (bottom diameter)
- glue (optional)

grapes fringe
- **12** pressed glass leaves
- 10g 4mm drop beads, in **1–3** colors
- 5 g 11º seed beads
- 5 g 14º or 15º seed beads

a

b

Art glass

Crystal drops

Floral fringe

Grape clusters and leaves

remaining beads and into the base. Exit the next end 8º.

3 Pick up three 4mm pearls, a 4mm spacer, a 4mm pearl, a 6mm pearl, a 4mm pearl, a 6mm pearl, a 4mm pearl, a 6mm pearl, and a 2mm bead. Skip the 2mm bead, and sew through the remaining beads and into the base. Secure the tail in the beadwork.

4 Repeat on the other end.

Floral Fringe

1 Pick up a bead cap, 40 11ºs, a leaf-shaped bead, and an 11º **(fig. 1, a–b)**. Skip the last 11º, and sew back through the leaf and the next four 11ºs **(b–c)**.

2 Pick up three 11ºs, a flower-shaped bead, and an 11º. Skip the 11º, and sew back through the flower and the next six 11ºs **(c–d)**.

3 Add leaves and flowers as desired in the same manner. When you finish the first fringe, sew back into the end round of the rope, and then exit the next 8º. Make a total of four fringes.

4 Secure the tail in the beadwork.

5 Repeat on the other end.

Grape Clusters and Leaves

1 Pick up 28 11ºs, four 15ºs, a 4mm drop bead, and three 15ºs **(fig. 2, a–b)**. Sew through the first 15º strung and on through the next two 11ºs **(b–c)**.

2 Pick up 23 15ºs, a drop, and two 15ºs **(c–d)**. Skip the last two 15ºs, the drop, and the next two 15ºs. Sew into the following two 15ºs, and pick up two 15ºs, a drop, and two 15ºs **(d–e)**. Sew through the next 15º **(e–f)**.

3 Continue, adding 19 drops as in step 2. When one cluster is completed, make four more clusters at even intervals along the base of 11ºs. Sew into the rope and exit the next 8º.

4 Pick up 27 11ºs, six 15ºs, a leaf bead, and five 15ºs **(fig. 3, a–b)**. Sew back through the first 15º added, and on through the next six 11ºs (b–c).

5 Pick up eight 15ºs, skip the last 15º, and sew through the remaining seven 15º. Then sew through the next five 11ºs **(c–d)**.

6 Pick up five 15ºs, a leaf, and six 15ºs. Sew though the next seven 11ºs **(d–e)**.

7 Repeat step 5 **(e–f)**. Pick up five 15ºs, skip the last 15º and sew through the remaining five 15º. Continue on through the next four 11ºs **(f–g)**.

8 Sew into the last row of the rope, and exit the next end 8º. Make two more fringes. Secure the tails, and trim. Repeat on the other end.

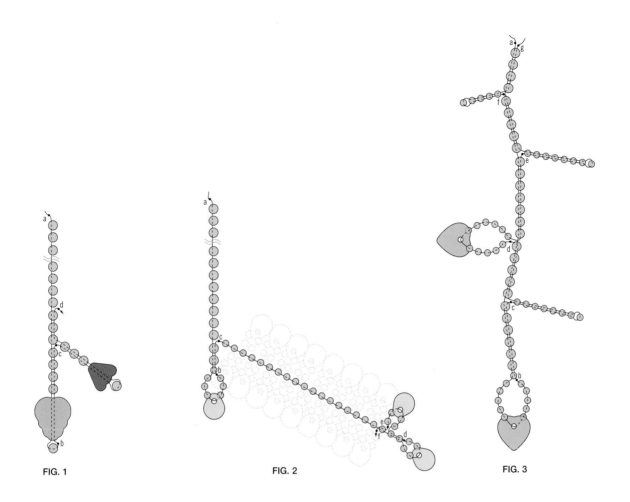

FIG. 1

FIG. 2

FIG. 3

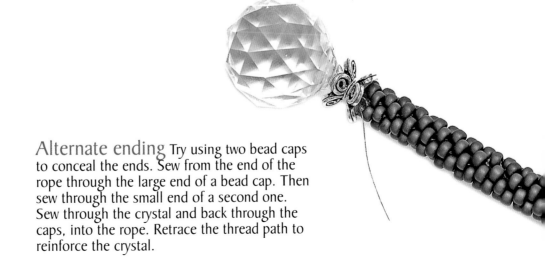

Alternate ending Try using two bead caps to conceal the ends. Sew from the end of the rope through the large end of a bead cap. Then sew through the small end of a second one. Sew through the crystal and back through the caps, into the rope. Retrace the thread path to reinforce the crystal.

Kumihimo Combination

If you love kumihimo and are looking for a new way to incorporate it into your beadwork, look no further. This clever combination of braiding and stitching fits the bill.

designed by Lisa Phillips

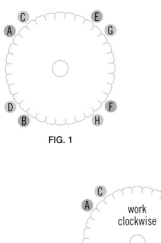

FIG. 1

work clockwise

FIG. 2

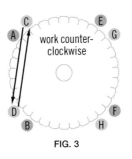

work counter-clockwise

FIG. 3

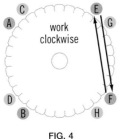

work clockwise

FIG. 4

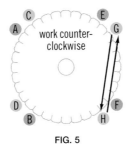

work counter-clockwise

FIG. 5

materials

necklace 18 in. (46cm)

- lampworked focal bead
- **48** 4–6mm Czech glass beads, color C
- **12–15** 4–6mm Czech glass beads in each of **2** colors: D and E
- 5 g 8º seed beads, color A
- 3 g 8º seed beads, color B
- 5 g 11º seed beads
- 3 g 15º seed beads
- clasp
- **2** cones or bead caps
- 3-in. (7.6cm) 14-gauge wire
- Fireline 6 or 8 lb. test
- 3 yd. (2.7m) fiber cord in each of **2** styles
- beading needles, #12
- anvil or bench block
- G-S Hypo Cement
- hammer
- marudai or kumihimo disk with **8** bobbins and counterweight
- metal file
- scrap wire or cord
- roundnose pliers
- wire cutters

Kumihimo Ladder Rope

I learned this rope from Jacqui Carey's book *Beads and Braids*. It creates a flat rope that has openings in it, like the gaps between the rungs of a ladder.

1 Cut two 1½-yd. (1.4m) pieces of each type of cord, for a total of four cords. Wind each end of each cord around a bobbin, leaving 10–12 in. (25–30cm) between the bobbins.

2 Position the two style A cords on the marudai or kumihimo disk so they are perpendicular and cross in the middle **(photo a)**. Move one notch to the right, and position the two style B cords so they are perpendicular and cross in the middle **(photo b)**. Tie or twist a piece of scrap cord or wire around the middle of all four cords where they cross. Attach the counterweight to the cord or wire.

3 Position the marudai or disk so the cords are arranged as in **fig. 1**. The cord positions are indicated by a letter, and you will always work with the cords in pairs: A and B, C and D, E and F, and G and H for the sides; and C and H and B and E for the rungs. If you are working on a marudai, grasp the first cord mentioned with your right hand and the other cord with your left hand, and move them simultaneously in the direction indicated for that movement. If you're working with a disk, pick up the first cord of the pair, move it in the direction indicated to the new position, then pick up the second cord, and move it in the direction indicated to the new position.

Begin the ladder rope as follows:

Movement 1: Working clockwise, move cord A to the cord B position, and move cord B to the cord A position **(fig. 2)**.

Movement 2: Working counterclockwise, move cord D to the cord C position, and move cord C to the cord D position **(fig. 3)**.

Movement 3: Working clockwise, move cord E to the cord F position, and move cord F to the cord E position **(fig. 4)**.

Movement 4: Working counterclockwise, move cord H to the cord G position, and move cord G to the cord H position **(fig. 5)**.

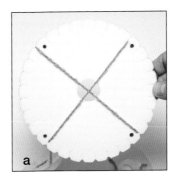

a

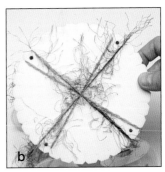

b

NOTE: You can use 20-gauge wire instead of 14-gauge to hang the focal bead, as shown here. Make a hook at the end, string the focal bead and a few spacers, and make a wrapped loop. After joining the spiral rope and braid, add a new thread at the middle of the spiral rope, and sew the loop to the beadwork. Cover the join with fringe. Art glass bead by Cathy Lybarger, aardvarkartglass.net.

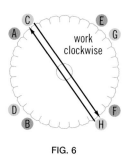

C — A — E — G

work clockwise

D — B — H — F

FIG. 6

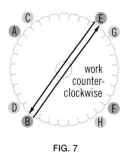

C — A — E — G

work counter-clockwise

D — B — H — F

FIG. 7

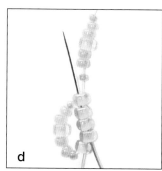

c

d

e

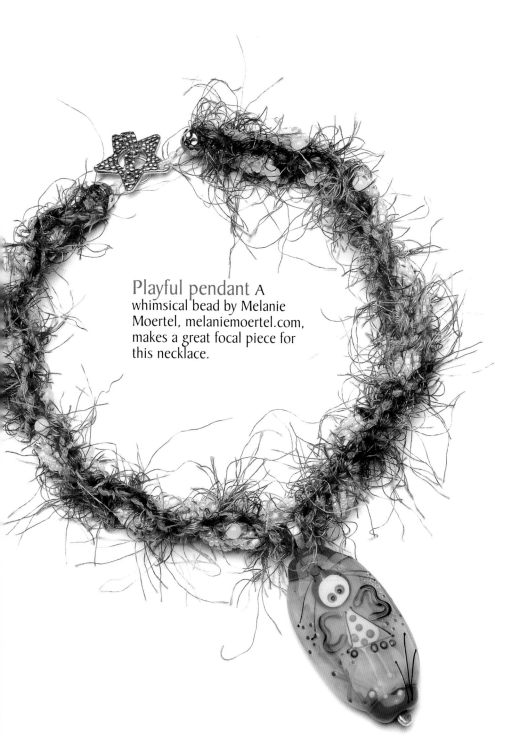

Playful pendant A whimsical bead by Melanie Moertel, melaniemoertel.com, makes a great focal piece for this necklace.

4 Repeat movements 1–4 three times. This creates two parallel braids that form the sides of an opening.

5 Make a ladder rung as follows:

Movement 5: Working clockwise, move cord C to the cord H position, and move cord H to the cord C position **(fig. 6)**.

Movement 6: Working counterclockwise, move cord B to the cord E position, and move cord E to the cord B position **(fig. 7)**.

6 Repeat movements 5 and 6 twice.

7 Continue as in steps 3–6 until the braid is 18 in. (46cm). Remove the braid from the marudai or disk, and tie the ends together with a tight square knot. Cut the cords close to the knot, apply glue to the knot, and set the braid aside.

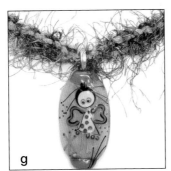

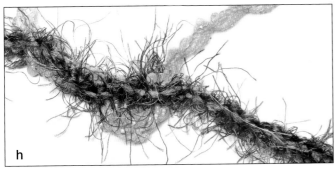

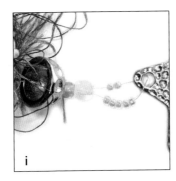

Spiral Rope

1 On 2 yd. (1.8m) of Fireline, leave an 8-in. (20cm) tail, and pick up four color A 8º seed beads, a 15º seed bead, two 11º seed beads, a color B 8º seed bead, two 11ºs, and a 15º. Sew through the 8ºs again **(photo c)**. The As are the core beads and the rest of the beads form a loop. Flip the loop to the left.

2 Pick up an A, a 15º two 11ºs, a B, two 11ºs, and a 15º, and sew through the top three As from the previous stitch and the A just added **(photo d)**. Pull tight to create a new loop, and flip it to the left so it sits on top of the previous loop. This bead sequence will be referred to as pattern 1.

3 Repeat step 2 13 times to make a pattern 1 segment with 15 loops.

4 Continue in spiral rope for three stitches, but pick up the following beads, which will be referred to as pattern 2:

First stitch: an A, a 15º, an 11º, a color C 4–6mm Czech glass bead, an 11º, and a 15º.

Second stitch: an A, a 15º, an 11º, a color D 4–6mm Czech glass bead, an 11º, and a 15.º

Third stitch: an A, a 15º, an 11º, a color C 4–6mm Czech glass bead, an 11º, and a 15.º

5 Work pattern 1 for four stitches.

6 Continue in spiral rope for three stitches as in pattern 2, but substitute a color E 4–6mm Czech glass bead for each D. This bead sequence will be referred to as pattern 3.

7 Work four pattern 1 stitches.

8 Work a repeating sequence of three pattern 2 stitches, four pattern 1 stitches, three pattern 3 stitches, and four pattern 1 stitches until you have 12 sets of both pattern 2 and pattern 3. End the rope with a total of 15

pattern 1 stitches. Do not end the thread.

Assembly

1 Cut a 3-in. (7.6cm) piece of 14-gauge wire. Place one end on the anvil or bench block, and hammer the end 1.8 in. (3mm) to flatten it **(photo e)**. Use a metal file to smooth the edges.

2 String the focal bead on the wire, then place the other end of the wire on the anvil or bench block, and hammer it flat, being careful not to hit the focal bead. Smooth the end with the file.

3 Use the widest part of your roundnose pliers to turn the end of the wire into a large loop **(photo f)**.

4 Center the pendant on the braid **(photo g)**.

5 Weave the spiral rope through the openings in the braid **(photo h)** until they are completely intertwined. Sew each end of the spiral rope to the ends of the braid.

6 On one end, pick up a cone, an 8º, a 4–6mm Czech glass bead, seven 15ºs, and half of the clasp. Sew back through the 4–6mm, the 8º, and the cone, and sew into the end of the braid **(photo i)**. Retrace the thread path to secure the clasp connection, and end the thread. Repeat at the other end.

Fabulous Fibers

designed by Gloria Farver

This lariat's soft braided rope is light and very wearable, yet stable enough to support a bounty of beaded dangles. Gather up your leftover beads and string them on headpins to turn them into dangles for fabulous fringe.

materials

lariat 1 yd. (.9m)

- **34–60** 3–6mm assorted accent beads
- **2** 4mm beads
- **2 g** 11° metal or glass seed beads
- **10** assorted silver beads or spacers
- **2** 8mm cones
- 12 in. (30cm) 22-gauge wire, half-hard
- 13 in. (33cm) cable chain, 3.6mm links
- **34** 2-in. (5cm) headpins
- 3 yd. (2.7m) each of **4** fibers
- **8** bobbins or pieces of card board
- braiding board or marudai
- glue
- weight
- chainnose pliers
- roundnose pliers
- wire cutters

a

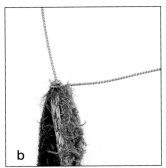

b

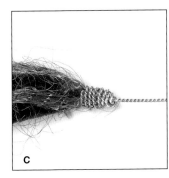

c

1 Cut a 12-in. (30cm) piece of wire in half. Use roundnose pliers to grasp one wire at its center, and make the first half of a wrapped loop **(photo a)**.

2 Center four 3-yd. (2.7m) fiber strands in the wire loop. Make a wrap at the base of the loop **(photo b)**, and continue wrapping over the loop and the fibers to secure them **(photo c)** instead of wrapping over the wire stem.

3 Position the wrapped loop in the center hole of the marudai or braiding board, and place a pair of fibers at the top, bottom, left, and right. Wrap the ends of the strands around bobbins or cardboard to keep them from tangling as you work **(photo d)**. Hanging a weight from the wire will keep the braid consistent by controlling the tension as you work.

4 Place the bottom two fibers between the top two fibers **(photo e)**.

5 Place the original top two fibers at the bottom **(photo f)**.

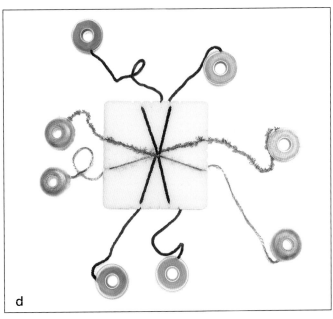

d

e

f

g

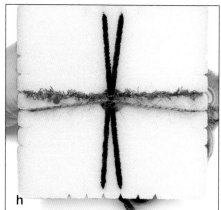

h

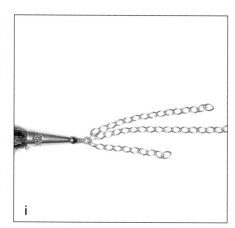

i

Most often made of wood, a marudai is a loom for freehand kumihimo braiding. To create tension, thread or yarn is rolled onto spools. A counterweight is placed at the base knot of these threads, where the rope begins.

6 Place the right two fibers between the left two fibers **(photo g)**.

7 Place the original left two fibers at the right **(photo h)**.

8 Repeat steps 4–7 until your lariat is the desired length. Remove the braided rope from the loom or braiding board and tie the loose ends in a square knot. Dot the knot with glue and allow it to dry.

9 Remove the weight, and slide a cone over the wire at the beginning of the lariat. Pick up a 4mm bead and make the first half of a wrapped loop.

10 Prepare the chain by cutting two 2½-in. (6.4cm) pieces, two 2-in. (5cm) pieces, and two 1½-in. (3.8cm) pieces. Slide one of each length of chain into the wire loop. Finish the wraps **(photo i)**.

11 String an assortment of accent beads on headpins, starting and ending with an 11º seed bead, and then make the first half of a wrapped loop **(photo j)**.

12 Attach a dangle to the end of one chain. Finish the wraps. Embellish every few links on each chain **(photo k)**.

13 On the remaining 6-in. (15cm) wire, make the first half of a wrapped loop. Slide the other end of the lariat, below the knot, into the loop **(photo l)**. Wrap the loop and remaining fibers. Trim the excess fibers. Attach a cone, a 4mm bead, chains, and dangles, as in steps 9–12 to complete the lariat.

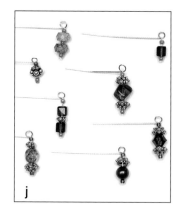

j

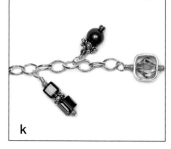

k

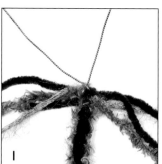

l

NOTE: Thinner fibers create narrower and more closely braided ropes. To make a thin-fiber lariat as long as its thicker-fiber counterpart, you will need to compensate by using longer strands.

Staggering Sparkle

Kumihimo worked with lentils and larger 8° seed beads creates a lush rope with plenty of depth and dimension.

designed by Rebecca Ann Combs

materials

- round foam kumihimo disk
- **8** weighted bobbins (approx. 23 grams each)
- center weight 1.6 oz. (45.4 grams)
- 12 yds. Superlon fine nylon string
- Big Eye needle
- **420** Crystal lentil beads
- Approx. 12 g 8º seed beads
- One-G, Nymo or other thin beading thread
- E6000 adhesive
- 8mm (inside diameter) magnetic endcap

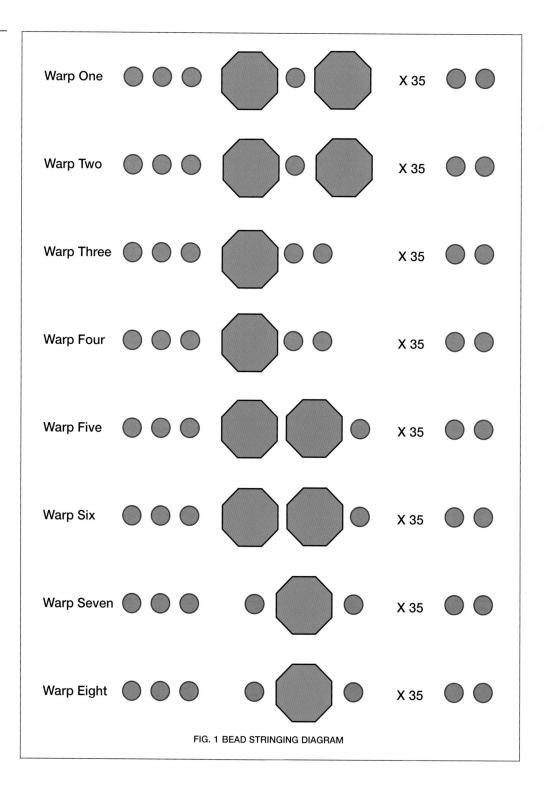

FIG. 1 BEAD STRINGING DIAGRAM

NOTE If you write on the metal washer, the number can be removed later with rubbing alcohol.

a

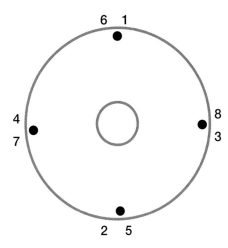

FIG. 2 BEAD STARTING DIAGRAM

Set Up

1 Cut eight 54-in. (1.4m) pieces of Superlon Fine and tie them together in an overhand knot. Use a permanent marker to number the weighted bobbins 1–8.

2 Use a Big Eye needle to string 11º seed beads onto each warp according to **fig. 1**. Tie a knot at the end of the string to keep the beads from falling off. Push the beads together as a group towards the disk so that they are about 2 in. (5cm) below it.

It is important to keep the beads together as a group so that they don't get tangled with the string. Starting at the loose end, wind the string and the beads onto the bobbin. Do this for each of the eight warps. It's OK if some of the crystals bulge out of the bobbin. At this point, all of the beads are below the disk. Leave an inch or so of working thread (empty string) between the underside of the disk and the start of the beads. Make sure that the numbered warps are arranged around the disk to

match **fig. 2**. Clip the center weight just below the knot. Compare yours to **photo a**.

Braid without Beads

Every beaded braid starts and ends with a short section without beads. This braided nubbin is where you'll bind and cut the braid.

1 Braid about a ½-in. (1.3cm) section without adding any beads using the Kongoh Gumi (basic round braid) braiding

sequence: Take the top-right cord and lift it out of its slot. Bring it straight down to the bottom-right and lock it next to the two cords that are already at the bottom. Remember—one warp per slot, no sharing. Notice that it starts on the right and finishes on the right. This is important. Cords in this braid only move vertically—straight up and down—never side to side or diagonally. See **fig. 3**.

Start

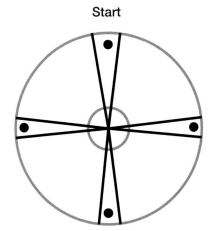

Top-Right Down

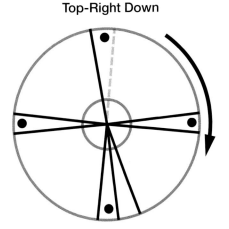

Bottom-Left Up

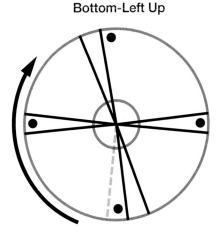

FIG. 3 BRAIDING SEQUENCE DIAGRAM

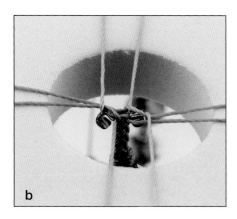

b

c

d

2 The next move is bottom-left up. Take the bottom-left cord and lift it out of its slot. Bring it straight up to the top-left and lock it next to the one cord that is already there. Again the rule is one warp per slot. Make sure that this left-side cord stays on the left and doesn't mistakenly get placed on the right. Many people find it helpful to use the right hand for right-side moves and the left hand for left-side moves. This can help prevent accidentally crossing the cords.

3 Rotate the disk a quarter turn counterclockwise. Repeat the "top-right down, bottom-left up, turn" braiding sequence until the braid is ½-in. long.

Braid with Beads

1 Because this is a counted pattern we want to start adding beads with warp number one. Keep braiding without beads until warp number one has returned to the top-right position and is ready to take its turn. This will be our first move with beads.

2 The braiding sequence remains the same with or without bead: top-right down, bottom-left up. The only difference is that every time you move a warp, you slide one bead into the middle of the braid. I use my index finger to slide one bead forward while my other fingers keep the rest of the beads back. Be sure to lock each bead into place by catching it on the first perpendicular warp that it crosses **(photo b)**. The first four beads are tricky. Go slowly and give the warp plenty of slack as you move it.

3 Add one bead to the braid every time you move a cord. The crystals are added in the same way by tucking them under the first perpendicular warp **(photo c)**. Continue braiding with beads until all of the beads have been added. Then braid a ½-in. section without beads.

Finishing

1 Braid another ½ in. without any beads. Remove the bobbins. Hold the point of braiding firmly under the disk and remove each warp from its slot. Tie all eight warps together using an overhand knot.

2 Bind the braid at each end as close as possible to the beads: Cut a piece of binding thread about 18 in. long. Fold it unevenly in half. Place the loop on top of the braid right next to the beads. Wrap the longer piece of thread around the braid and the thread tail three or four times. Bring the working thread through the loop. Pull the tail to close the loop. Make an extra little square knot on top for good measure **(photo d)**.

3 Trim the tails close to the knot. Cut off the nubbin very close to the binding, and glue an endcap to each end of the braid **(photo e)**. The endcap will fit over the beads **(photo f)**. Let the glue dry 24 hours.

Silver streak Crystal lentil beads give this elegant necklace texture and sparkle for eye-catching style.

Basics

THREAD AND KNOTS
Adding thread

To add a thread, sew into the beadwork several rows or rounds prior to the point where the last bead was added, leaving a short tail. Follow the thread path of the stitch, tying a few half-hitch knots (see "Half-hitch knot") between beads as you go, and exit where the last stitch ended. Trim the short tail.

Conditioning thread

Use beeswax or microcrystalline wax or Thread Heaven to condition nylon beading thread and Fireline. Wax smooths nylon fibers and adds tackiness that will stiffen your beadwork slightly. Thread Heaven adds a static charge that causes the thread to repel itself, so don't use it with doubled thread. Both conditioners help thread resist wear. To condition, stretch nylon thread to remove the curl (Fireline doesn't stretch). Lay the thread or Fireline on top of the conditioner, hold it in place with your thumb or finger, and pull the thread through the conditioner.

Ending thread

To end a thread, sew back through the last few rows or rounds of beadwork, following the thread path of the stitch and tying two or three half-hitch knots (see "Half-hitch knot") between beads as you go. Sew through a few beads after the last knot, and trim the thread.

Half-hitch knot

Pass the needle under the thread bridge between two beads, and pull gently until a loop forms. Cross back over the thread between the beads, sew through the loop, and pull gently to draw the knot into the beadwork.

Overhand knot

Make a loop with the thread. Pull the tail through the loop, and tighten.

Square knot

1 Cross one end of the thread over and under the other end. Pull both ends to tighten the first half of the knot.

2 Cross the first end of the thread over and under the other end. Pull both ends to tighten the knot.

Stop bead

Use a stop bead to secure beads temporarily when you begin stitching. Choose a bead that is different from the beads in your project. Pick up the stop bead, leaving the desired length tail. Sew through the stop bead again in the same direction, making sure you don't split the thread. If desired, sew through it one more time for added security.

Surgeon's knot

1 Cross one end of the thread over and under the other twice. Pull both ends to tighten the first half of the knot.

2 Cross the first end of the thread over and under the other end. Pull both ends to tighten the knot.

CROCHET
Steel crochet hooks

Bead crochet ropes are usually worked with steel crochet hooks, which are short hooks (about 5 in./13cm long) with very small heads (about 1–3mm).

Today's steel hooks are marked with a size (00–14, with the head getting smaller as the size number gets higher) and a metric measurement. As seen in the chart below, however, hook manufacturers aren't consistent in their use of size numbers. So whenever possible, choose your hook based on the metric measurement.

A bead crochet project will usually specify a hook size, which is determined by the thread used. The thinner the thread, the smaller the hook you'll need. However, individual stitching tension is also a factor, and you may find you need to deviate from the suggested hook size.

	Metric measurement (in mm)	
	Bates	Boye
00	2.7	3.5
0	2.55	3.25
1	2.35	2.75
2	2.20	2.25
3	2.0	2.1
4	1.75	2.0
5	1.7	1.9
6	1.6	1.8
7	1.5	1.65
8	1.4	1.5
9	1.25	1.4
10	1.15	1.3
11	1.05	1.1
12	1.0	1.0
13	.95	.85
14	.9	.75

(U.S. size shown along left column axis, 00–14)

Basics

Slip knot and chain stitch

1 Make a slip knot: Leaving the desired length tail, make a loop in the cord, crossing the spool end over the tail. Insert the hook in the loop, yarn over, and pull the cord through the loop.

2 Yarn over the hook, and draw through the loop. Repeat this step for the desired number of chain stitches.

Bead crochet methods

When worked in bead slip stitch, the beads nestle much like in peyote stitch.

When worked in bead single crochet with the bead added in the first yarn over, the beads line up at an angle.

When worked in bead single crochet with the bead added in the second yarn over, the beads line up more vertically.

Bead crochet ropes

It can be helpful to work in a repeating pattern to easily see what stitch your hook should be going into. This five-around rope uses a different bead color for each stitch.

1 String the beads for your project onto the cord. Do not cut the cord from the spool—wind the strung beads around the spool and unwind them as you work.

2 Leaving a 10-in. (25cm) tail, work five bead chain stitches **(photo a)**. Use a bead slip stitch to join it into a ring: Insert the hook to the left of the bead in the first chain, flipping the bead to the right **(photo b)**. Slide the next bead to the hook. Yarn over **(photo c)**, and pull through both the stitch and the loop on the hook **(photo d)**. This is the first stitch of the next round.

a

b

c

d

3 Continue working in bead slip stitch around the ring, working each stitch into the loop of cord that attaches the next bead in the previous round. If you used a different color for each bead in the round, each stitch will be worked in a stitch with the same color bead. Work to the desired length. Cut the cord, leaving a 6-in. (15cm) tail.

Invisible join

The following method can be used with a slip stitch bead crochet rope of any bead count diameter. The instructions below refer to a five-around rope, but if you make a six-around rope, for example, adjust the counts in the instructions accordingly.

1 To bury the ending tail, attach a tapestry or other needle, and carefully sew through the two loops of the last stitch and into the middle of the rope, exiting between two beads several rounds into the work. Sew back and forth through the rope several times, crossing over the cord within the rope without sewing through any beads, and trim the cord as close to the beadwork as possible.

2 Attach a tapestry needle to the beginning tail, which is exiting the first stitch in the first round. Identify the five beads added in the final round and the five beads in the first round. The beads in the final round lie sideways because they haven't yet been locked in place.

3 Line up the ends of the rope, aligning the pattern. On the tail end of the rope, sew under the loop of the fifth bead from the end. Flip the bead to the right as you would while crocheting **(photo e)**. Notice that this bead is the same color as the one your cord just came from at the other end of the rope.

e

4 At the beginning end of the rope, sew under the loop of the second bead in the first round **(photo f)**, sewing toward the third bead.

5 Cross over to the tail end again, and sew under the fourth bead from the end of the round **(photo g)**.

6 Continue working back and forth between the ends, flipping the beads in the final round, and matching up the pattern. After you've flipped the end bead on the tail end, sew under the first bead at the beginning end again. End the tail as in step 1, and trim.

BEAD CROCHET BASICS

Bead chain stitch

1 Make a loop in the thread, crossing the ball end over the tail. Insert the hook in the loop, yarn over the hook **(fig. 1)**, and pull through the loop.
2 Slide a bead down to the hook. Yarn over the hook **(fig. 2)**, and draw through the loop. Repeat for the desired number of chain stitches. The bead chain should curl into the shape of a backwards comma **(fig. 3)**.

Forming a ring

Insert the hook to the left of the bead in the first stitch. Flip the bead to the right, and slide a bead to the hook. Yarn over **(fig. 4)**, and pull through both loops on the hook.

Bead slip stitch

1 Insert the hook to the left of the next bead, and flip that bead to the right **(fig. 5)**.
2 Slide a bead down to the hook, yarn over **(fig. 6)**, and pull through both the stitch and the loop on the hook.

Bead single crochet

Bead single crochet can be worked both flat and in the round. To work bead single crochet, begin with a chain, with or without beads.

1 Insert the hook into the two loops of the next stitch in the previous row or round.

2 Slide a bead up to the hook, yarn over, and pull through the two loops **(figs. 7 and 8)**.
3 Yarn over, and pull through the remaining loops on the hook **(figs. 9 and 10)**.

You can alter the results somewhat by making some slight changes. For example, you can insert your hook into only the top or bottom loop, though in tubular crochet it can be difficult to distinguish individual loops because they're somewhat buried inside the tube. Furthermore, you can add your bead in the second yarn over instead of the first. Experiment to find your favorite style.

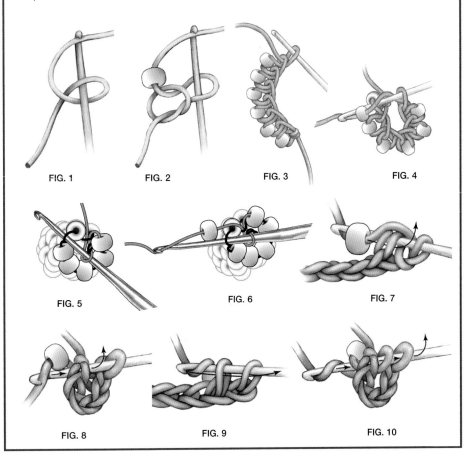

FIG. 1   FIG. 2   FIG. 3   FIG. 4

FIG. 5   FIG. 6   FIG. 7

FIG. 8   FIG. 9   FIG. 10

Basics

HERRINGBONE STITCH

Flat herringbone

1 Work the first row in ladder stitch (see "Ladder stitch") to the desired length, exiting the top of an end bead in the ladder.

2 Pick up two beads, and sew down through the next bead in the previous row (**a–b**). Sew up through the following bead in the previous row, pick up two beads, and sew down through the next bead (**b–c**). Repeat across the first row.

3 To turn to start the next row, sew down through the end bead in the previous row and back through the last bead of the pair just added (**a–b**). Pick up two beads, sew down through the next bead in the previous row, and sew up through the following bead (**b–c**). Continue adding pairs of beads across the row.

Tubular herringbone

Tubular herringbone starts from a ladder of beads formed into a ring, or with a simple ring of beads. In either case, begin with an even number of beads. Once you get started, you can choose to make the ribs of the stitch straight (**photo a**) or twisted (**photo b**).

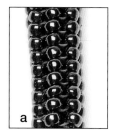

Straight tubular herringbone

For a ladder start, stitch a ladder with an even number of beads and form it into a ring. Your thread should exit the top of a bead. Pick up two beads, and sew down through the next bead in the previous round (**fig. 1, a–b**). Sew up through the next bead, and repeat around the ring to complete the round (**b–c**).

FIG. 1

You will need to step up to start the next round. Sew up through two beads—the next bead in the previous round and the first bead added in the new round (**c–d**).

Alternatively, begin by picking up four beads, and sew through them again to form a ring. Sew through the first bead again, and snug up the beads (**fig. 2, a–b**). Pick up two beads and sew through the next bead (**b–c**). Repeat three times, and step up through the first bead picked up in this round (**c–d**).

FIG. 2

Whether you began with a ladder or a ring, continue adding two beads per stitch. As you work, snug up the beads to form a tube, and step up at the end of each round until your rope is the desired length.

Twisted tubular herringbone

Form a base ring with an even number of beads. Pick up two beads, and sew through the next bead in the previous round (**fig. 3, a–b**). Sew up through the next bead, and repeat around the ring to complete the round (**b–c**).

You will need to step up to start the next round. Sew up through two beads—the bead from the previous round and the first bead added in the new round (**c–d**). Work one round of straight herringbone (**d–e**).

To create a twist in the tube, pick up two beads, sew down through one bead in the next stack and up through two beads in the following stack (**e–f**). Repeat around the ring, adding two beads per stitch. Step up to the next round through three beads (**f–g**). Snug up the beads to form a tube. The twist will begin to appear after the sixth round. Continue until your rope is the desired length.

To create a twist in the other direction, work the first two rounds as described. Pick up two beads, sew down through two beads in the next stack, and up through one bead in the following stack. Repeat around the ring, adding two beads per stitch. Step up to the next round through two beads.

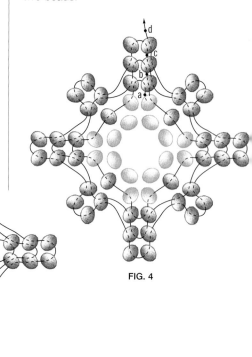

FIG. 4

FIG. 3

Increasing in tubular herringbone

Increases are usually made between stitches. In the first increase round, pick up a single bead between the stitches **(fig. 4, a–b)**. You will not stitch through these single beads; they are used to fill in the space between rounds. In the next round, pick up two beads between the pairs of beads **(b–c)**. In subsequent rounds, work in tubular herringbone with the increase pairs as bases for new stacks of beads **(c–d)**. The increase stacks may initially seem shorter than the other stacks, but they will catch up as you work additional rounds.

LADDER STITCH

Making a ladder

1 Pick up two beads, and sew through them both again, positioning the beads side by side so that their holes are parallel **(fig. 1)**.

FIG. 1

2 Add subsequent beads by picking up one bead, sewing through the previous bead, then sewing through the new bead **(fig. 2)**. Continue for the desired length.

FIG. 2

This technique produces uneven tension, which you can correct by zigzagging back through the beads in the opposite direction or by choosing the "Crossweave method" or "Alternative method."

Crossweave technique

1 Thread a needle on each end of a length of thread, and center a bead.

2 Working in cross-weave technique, pick up a bead with one needle, and cross the other needle through it **(fig. 3 a–b)** and **(c–d)**. Add all subsequent beads in the same manner.

FIG. 3

Alternative method

1 Pick up all the beads you need for the length of your project. Fold the last two beads so they are parallel, and sew through the second-to-last bead again in the same direction **(fig. 4)**.

FIG. 4

2 Fold the next loose bead so it sits parallel to the previous bead in the ladder, and sew through the loose bead in the same direction **(fig. 5)**. Continue sewing back through each bead until you exit the last bead of the ladder.

FIG. 5

Forming a ring

With your thread exiting the last bead in the ladder, sew through the first bead and then through the last bead again. If using the "Crossweave method" or "Alternative method" of ladder stitch, cross the threads from the last bead in the ladder through the first bead in the ladder.

RIGHT-ANGLE WEAVE

Flat strip

1 To start the first row of right-angle weave, pick up four beads, and tie them into a ring (see "Square knot") **(fig. 1)**. Sew through the first three beads again.

FIG. 1

2 Pick up three beads. Sew through the last bead in the previous stitch **(fig. 2 a–b)**, and continue through the first two beads picked up in this stitch **(b–c)**.

FIG. 2

3 Continue adding three beads per stitch until the first row is the desired length **(fig. 3)**. You are stitching in a figure-8 pattern, alternating the direction of the thread path for each stitch.

FIG. 3

Adding rows

1 To add a row, sew through the last stitch of row 1, exiting an edge bead along one side **(fig. 4)**.

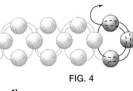

FIG. 4

2 Pick up three beads, and sew through the edge bead your thread exited in the previous step **(fig. 5 a–b)**. Continue through the first new bead **(b–c)**.

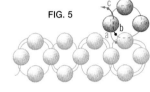

FIG. 5

3 Pick up two beads, and sew back through the next edge bead in the previous row and the bead your thread exited at the start of this step **(fig. 6 a–b)**. Continue through the two new beads and the following edge bead in the previous row **(b–c)**.

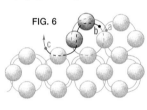

FIG. 6

4 Pick up two beads, and sew through the last two beads your thread exited in the previous stitch and the first new bead. Continue working a figure-8 thread path, picking up two beads per stitch for the rest of the row **(fig. 7)**.

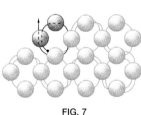

FIG. 7

Forming a strip into a ring

Exit the end bead of the last stitch, pick up a bead, and sew through the end bead of the first stitch. Pick up a bead, and sew through the end bead of the last stitch.

Basics

PEYOTE STITCH

Flat Even-Count

1 Pick up an even number of beads, leaving the desired 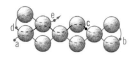 length tail **(a–b)**. These beads will shift to form the first two rows as the third row is added.

2 To begin row 3, pick up a bead, skip the last bead added in the previous step, and sew back through the next bead, working toward the tail **(b–c)**. For each stitch, pick up a bead, skip a bead in the previous row, and sew through the next bead until you reach the first bead picked up in step 1 **(c–d)**. The beads added in this row are higher than the previous rows and are referred to as "up-beads."

3 For each stitch in subsequent rows, pick up a bead, and sew through the next up-bead in the previous row **(d–e)**. To count peyote stitch rows, add the total number of beads along both straight edges.

Flat odd-count

Odd-count peyote is the same as even-count peyote, except for the turn on odd-numbered rows, where the last bead of the row can't be attached in the usual way because there is no up-bead to sew through.

1 Begin as for flat even-count peyote, but pick up an odd number of beads. Work row 3 as in even-count, stopping before adding the last bead.

2 Work a figure-8 turn at the end of row 3: Sew through the first bead picked up in step 1 (bead #1). 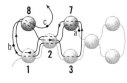 Pick up the last bead of the row you're working on (bead #8), and sew through beads #2, #3, #7, #2, #1, and #8. You can work the

figure-8 turn at the end of each odd-numbered row, but this will cause this edge to be stiffer than the other. Instead, in subsequent odd-numbered rows, pick up the last bead of the row, sew under the thread bridge between the last two 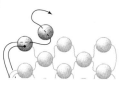 edge beads, and sew back through the last bead added to begin the next row.

Tubular

Tubular peyote stitch follows the same stitching pattern as flat peyote, but instead of sewing back and forth, you work in rounds.

1 Pick up an even number of beads, and tie them into a ring with a square knot, leaving the desired length tail. If desired, slide the ring onto a dowel.

2 Sew through the first bead in the ring. Pick up a bead, skip a bead in the ring, and sew through the next bead. Repeat to complete the round.

3 To step up to start the next round, sew through the first bead added in this round **(a–b)**.

4 Pick up a bead, and sew through the next bead in round 3 **(b–c)**. Repeat this stitch to complete the round.

5 Repeat steps 3 and 4 for the desired length tube.

Circular

Circular peyote is also worked in continuous rounds like tubular peyote, but the rounds stay flat and radiate outward from the center as a result of increases or using larger beads. If the rounds do not increase, the edges will curve upward.

Zipping up or joining

To join two pieces of flat peyote invisibly, match up the two pieces so the end rows fit together. "Zip up" the pieces by zigzagging through the up-beads on both ends.

BRICK STITCH

1 Work the first row in ladder stitch (see "Ladder stitch: Making a ladder") to the desired length, exiting the top of the last bead added.

2 Pick up two beads, sew under the thread bridge between the second and third beads in the previous row, and sew back up through the second bead added. To secure this first stitch, sew down through the first bead and back up through the second bead. The first stitch in the new row will be centered above the second bead in the previous row.

3 For the remaining stitches in the row, pick up one bead per stitch, sew under the thread bridge between the next two beads in the previous row, and sew back up through the new bead. The last stitch in the new row will be centered above the second-to-last bead in the previous row, and the new row will be one bead shorter than the previous row, unless you work an increase.

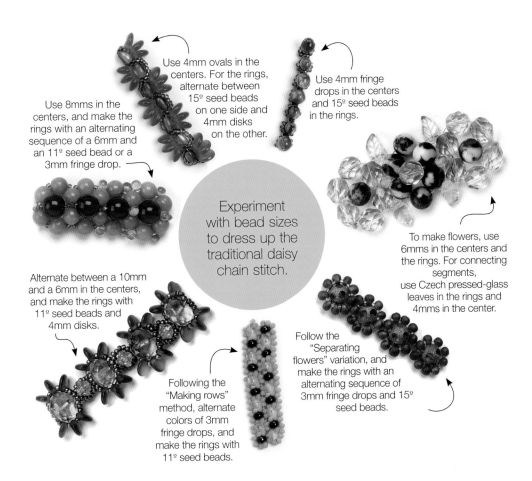

Use 4mm ovals in the centers. For the rings, alternate between 15º seed beads on one side and 4mm disks on the other.

Use 8mms in the centers, and make the rings with an alternating sequence of a 6mm and an 11º seed bead or a 3mm fringe drop.

Use 4mm fringe drops in the centers and 15º seed beads in the rings.

Experiment with bead sizes to dress up the traditional daisy chain stitch.

To make flowers, use 6mms in the centers and the rings. For connecting segments, use Czech pressed-glass leaves in the rings and 4mms in the center.

Alternate between a 10mm and a 6mm in the centers, and make the rings with 11º seed beads and 4mm disks.

Following the "Making rows" method, alternate colors of 3mm fringe drops, and make the rings with 11º seed beads.

Follow the "Separating flowers" variation, and make the rings with an alternating sequence of 3mm fringe drops and 15º seed beads.

DAISY CHAIN

Daisy chain bears some similarity to right-angle weave because beads of the previous stitch are shared to create the next stitch, and the stitches are worked in rounds. Daisy chain creates a ring of beads around a single bead. The most basic version uses six seed beads to form the ring, with a seventh seed bead in the center. When using one color bead in the center and a second color for the ring of beads, the stitch looks like a chain of daisies. Each flower shares a pair of petals with the next flower, so the chain is linked by pairs of beads.

Change the look by changing the number, size, or shape of beads you use. The stitch can also be modified to separate the flowers or to create rows of flowers.

Daisy chain can be worked in two ways: starting with a ring and then adding the center, or starting with half of a ring, adding the center, and finishing the other half of the ring.

The following instructions show both methods using 11º seed beads. When substituting bead sizes, be sure to use enough beads in the ring to surround the center bead.

Methods
Start with a ring

1 Pick up six color A 11º seed beads. To create a ring, sew through the first A picked up **(fig. 1, a–b)**.

FIG. 1

2 Pick up a color B 11º seed bead, and sew through the A opposite the A your thread exited at the start of this step **(b–c)**.

3 Pick up four As, and sew through the A adjacent to the A your thread exited at the start of this step **(c–d)**.

4 Pick up a B, and sew through the A opposite the A your thread exited at the start of this step **(d–e)**.

5 Repeat steps 3 and 4 to make the chain the desired length. Start with half of a ring

Start with half of a ring

1 Pick up four color A 11º seed beads and a color B 11º seed bead, and sew back through the first A **(fig. 2, a–b)**.

FIG. 2

2 Pick up two As, and sew through the last A picked up before the B in step 1 **(b–c)**.

Basics

3 Pick up two As and a B, and sew through the last A picked up in the previous stitch **(c–d)**.

4 Pick up two As, and sew through the last A picked up in the previous stitch **(d–e)**.

5 Repeat steps 3 and 4 to make the chain the desired length.

Variations
Separating flowers

1 Work the first stitch as in steps 1 and 2 of your preferred method.

2 Pick up two 11ºs, and sew through the two corresponding 11ºs in the previous stitch and the two 11ºs just picked up **(fig. 3, a–b)**.

3 Work the next stitch as in steps 3 and 4 of your preferred method **(b–c)**.

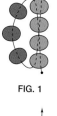

FIG. 3

4 Repeat steps 2 and 3 to make the chain the desired length.

Making Rows

Choose your preferred method. These instructions use "Start with half of a ring."

1 Work a row of daisy chain to the desired length using eight 11º seed beads for the rings and a 3mm fringe drop in each center **(fig. 4, a–b)**.

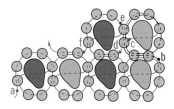

FIG. 4

2 To step up, sew through the next two 11ºs. Pick up six 11ºs, and sew through

the last two 11ºs from the previous stitch and the first 11º picked up in this step **(b–c)**.

3 Pick up a 3mm, and sew through the opposite 11º in the ring and the next four 11ºs **(c–d)**.

4 Sew through the top pair of 11ºs in the next stitch of the previous row, pick up an 11º and a 3mm, and sew through the adjacent 11º to the 11º your thread exited at the start of this step **(d–e)**.

5 Pick up three 11ºs, and sew through the first 11º picked up in step 4 **(e–f)**.

6 Repeat steps 4 and 5 for the length of the row.

SPIRAL
Spiral rope

The spiral rope has a core of beads around which loops of beads rotate.

1 On a comfortable length of thread, pick up four color A and three color B 11º seed beads, and sew through the four As again **(fig. 1)**, leaving a 6-in. (15cm) tail. The Bs will create a small loop. Move the loop to the left of the As.

FIG. 1

FIG. 2

2 Pick up an A and three Bs, and sew through the top three As from the previous stitch and the new A added in this stitch **(fig. 2)**. Push the new loop of Bs to the left so it rests on top of the previous loop.

3 Repeat step 2 for the desired rope length.

There are numerous ways to vary the spiral rope. Try making:

• loops with an 11º, a 4mm pearl or crystal, and an 11º.

• loops with an 11º, a 6mm offset-hole lentil bead, and an 11º.

• a double spiral in which a second set of loops is added in the groove created by the first set of loops.

Russian Spiral

Russian spiral is a variant of tubular netting. It is usually stitched with beads in two sizes—often two sizes of seed beads, or seed beads and either bugle beads or crystals—resulting in alternating stripes circling the tube.

1 On a comfortable length of thread, pick up a repeating pattern of two 11º seed beads and an 8º seed bead three times, and tie the beads into a ring with a square knot, leaving a 6-in. (15cm) tail. Sew through the first 11º again **(fig. 3)**.

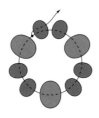

FIG. 3

2 Pick up an 8º and two 11ºs, and sew through the 11º right after the next 8º **(fig. 4, a–b)**. Repeat **(b–c)**. Repeat again, and step up through the first two beads added in this round **(c–d)**.

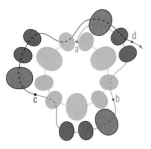

FIG. 4

3 Repeat step 2 **(fig. 5)** for the desired rope length.

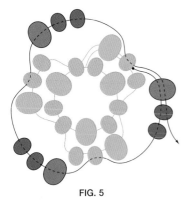

FIG. 5

Many different combinations of beads will work in this stitch, as shown here:

• a variation with two 15ºs substituted for the 11ºs and a 3mm bugle for the 8º.

• a pearl variation with three 11ºs instead of two and a 4mm pearl instead of the 8º.

• a multicolor variation with three 11ºs instead of two, and a rotating pattern of a 4mm crystal, a 4mm glass bead, or a 4mm pearl instead of the 8ºs.

Cellini spiral

Cellini spiral is a variant of tubular peyote. The undulating spiral is created by a progression of bead sizes, from small beads to large beads and then back to small beads. It creates a fairly stiff piece of sculptural beadwork. Keep tight tension to avoid thread showing between the transition from larger to smaller beads.

Cellini spiral sample

1 On a comfortable length of thread, pick up two color A 15º seed beads, two color B 15º seed beads, two color C 11º cylinder beads, two color D 11º seed beads, two color E 8º seed beads, two Ds, and two Cs. Tie the beads into a ring with a square knot, and sew through the first two As again **(fig. 1, a–b)**. This bead sequence makes up the first two rounds of peyote.

materials

samples

• 1–3 g each of **4** sizes of beads:

• 15º seed beads in each of **2** colors: A, B

• 11º cylinder beads, color C

• 11º seed beads, color D

• 8º seed beads, color E (spiral sample only)

• Fireline 6 lb. test, or nylon beading thread, size D

• beading needles, #12

2 Working in tubular peyote stitch, pick up the following beads, one per stitch: A, B, C, D, E, D, C. Step up through the first A in the new round **(b–c)**.

3 Repeat step 2 **(fig. 2)** to the desired length.

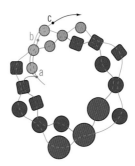

FIG. 1

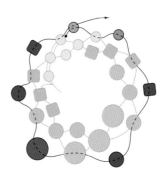

FIG.2

Basics

STRINGING & WIREWORK

Opening and closing loops and jump rings

1 Hold a loop or a jump ring with two pairs of pliers, such as chainnose, flatnose, or bentnose pliers.

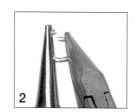

2 To open the loop or jump ring, bring the tips of one pair of pliers toward you, and push the tips of the other pair away from you.

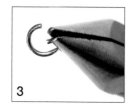

3 The open jump ring. Reverse the steps to close.

Plain loop

1 Using chainnose pliers, make a right-angle bend in the wire directly above a bead or other component or at least ¼ in. (6mm) from the end of a naked piece of wire. For a larger loop, bend the wire further in.

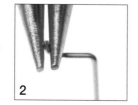

2 Grip the end of the wire with roundnose pliers so that the wire is flush with the jaws of the pliers where they meet. The closer to the tip of the pliers

that you work, the smaller the loop will be. Press downward slightly, and rotate the wire toward the bend made in step 1.

3 Reposition the pliers in the loop to continue rotating the wire until the end of the wire touches the bend.

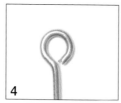

4 The plain loop.

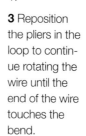

Wrapped loop

1 Using chainnose pliers, make a right-angle bend in the wire about 2mm above a bead or other component or at least 1¼ in. (3.2cm) from the end of a naked piece of wire.

2 Position the jaws of the roundnose pliers in the bend. The closer to the tip of the pliers that you work, the smaller the loop will be.

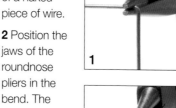

3 Curve the short end of the wire over the top jaw of the roundnose pliers.

4 Reposition the pliers so the lower jaw fits snugly in the loop. Curve the wire downward around the bottom jaw of the pliers. This is the first half of a wrapped loop.

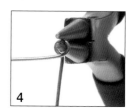

5 To complete the wraps, grasp the top of the loop with one pair of pliers.

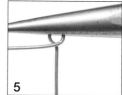

6 With another pair of pliers, wrap the wire around the stem two or three times. Trim the excess wire, and gently press the cut end close to the wraps with chainnose pliers.

Contributors

Contact **Michelle Bevington** via e-mail at beadart@rain.org.

Carolyn Cave is a self-taught bead artist, wife, mother of three, and musician living in Alberta. She is the author of *Beautiful Designs with SuperDuos and Twin Beads* (Kalmbach Books). See Carolyn's work on her Facebook page, Lady Beadle Designs.

Mary Carroll is a graphic designer and self-taught beaded jewelry designer who resides near Denver, Colo. Contact Mary via e-mail at dmcarroll@renegadegraphics.biz.

Rebecca Ann Combs has always had a passion for creating and teaching. She is the owner of Design & Adorn Beading Studio in Tucson, Ariz., and author of *Kumihimo Basics & Beyond* (Kalmbach Books). Visit designnandadorn.com/rebecca-combs.

Jane Danley Cruz has been beading for more than 20 years. She lives in Waukesha, Wis., and is a former associate editor at *Bead&Button* magazine. Contact her at jmdcruz262@gmail.com.

Mary DiMatteo is a designer and teacher from Florida. Contact her via e-mail at mdimatteo@bellsouth.net.

Anna Elizabeth Draeger is a jewelry designer, former associate editor for *Bead&Button* magazine, and the author of the books *Crystal Brilliance, Creative Designs Using Shaped Beads,* and *Crystal Play* (Kalmbach Books). Visit her website, originaldesignsbyanna.squarespace.com.

Susan Yvette England has been a potter and artist since 1991, and began jewelry making in 2003. Contact her via e-mail at earthelementsart@aol.com.

Gloria Farver has been beading for over 10 years. Gloria also enjoys knitting, gardening, and spending time with her grandson in Brookfield, Wis. Contact Gloria via e-mail at rfarver@wi.rr.com.

Julia Gerlach is the editor at Bead&Button magazine in Waukesha, Wis. Contact her in care of *Bead&Button*.

Linda Gettings, of Center Valley, Pa., is a full-time jewelry designer, teacher, and writer. She has been teaching beadweaving and wirework for over 20 years. Visit her website, bead-patterns.com.

Lisa Keith's current favorite techniques include right-angle weave, herringbone, and unique tribal stitches. Contact her in care of Kalmbach Books at books@kalmbach.com.

Isabella Lam and her husband, Avi, currently live in Israel and together own the bead shop "Hut Hashani," where they sell her DIY kits and booklets. Visit her website, isabellalam.com.

Rona Loomis, of N.Y., is a jewelry artisan who specializes in bead crochet. Contact her via e-mail at beadedswan@aol.com, or visit her website, beadedswan.com.

Carol Perrenoud is an internationally recognized bead artist, teacher, and entrepreneur whose work has been widely exhibited and featured. Contact Carol via e-mail at carol@beadcats.com, or visit her website, beadcats.com.

Lisa Phillips was an avid beader who especially enjoyed mixing fibers and beads in a variety of ways. Direct questions about Lisa's project to Kalmbach Books at books@kalmbach.com.com.

Karen Price, of Ontario, calls herself a student of beading. She loves trying new techniques and projects. Contact Karen via e-mail at kap0002@hotmail.com.

Adele Rogers Recklies is the author of *Bead Crochet Snakes: History and Technique*. Adele also embroiders, crochets, and knits costumes for a variety of performances, including Broadway shows. Visit her website, beadcrochetsnakes.com, or her blog, recklessbeadingblogspot.com.

Keiko Seki, of Japan, became interested in beading when a friend gave her a piece of handmade beaded jewelry, and now enjoys giving her jewelry to others. Contact Keiko in care of Kalmbach Books via e-mail at books@kalmbach.com.

Beth Stone, of West Bloomfield, Mich., has a passion for beads and a creative, inquisitive approach to bead stitching. She is the author of *Seed Bead Stitching, More Seed Bead Stitching, Bead, Play & Love,* and the upcoming *Bead Play Everyday*. Contact Beth via e-mail at bnshdl@msn.com.

Julie Walker, of Dayton, Ohio, has been designing jewelry for over 15 years. She is the former owner of The Bead Cage. Visit her Etsy shop, etsy.com/shop/beadymarket.

Jill Wiseman is the author of *Jill Wiseman's Beautiful Beaded Ropes*, and a full-time beadweaving designer and national instructor. Contact her via e-mail at jill@tapestrybeads.com, or visit her website, tapestrybeads.com.

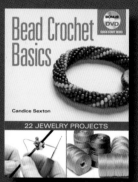
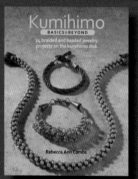
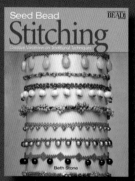